THOMAS PERCY & JOHN BOWLE

CERVANTINE CORRESPONDENCE

Edited by

Daniel Eisenberg

The Florida State University

UNIVERSITY OF EXETER

1987

ISSN 0305 8700

ISBN 0 85989 288 3

314704

Printed by

Short Run Press Ltd, Exeter

March 1987

INTRODUCTION

This volume contains the surviving letters exchanged by two eighteenth-century scholars, John Bowle and Thomas Percy. Except for three of Bowle´s letters held by the British Library in Additional MS 32329 (Nos 44, 46, and 48 of the present volume), all of them are part of the Bowle-Evans collection in the library of the University of Cape Town.

The Bowle-Evans collection, described by R. F. M. Immelman,[1] was purchased by the University of Cape Town in 1957 from a descendant of Bowle. It includes a catalog of his substantial library, a portion of it (though not the Spanish section, long dispersed), and two volumes of his correspondence, source of the present edition. More specifically, the letters of Percy are contained in the Epistolarium Bowleanum, into which Bowle pasted letters received. From the contents of the letters we can conclude that the collection of those received from Percy is nearly complete.

Bowle´s letters to Percy are found in Bowle´s Green Book, which begins in 1772, five years after the first letter from Percy; Bowle´s earlier letters are apparently lost. From the extensive revision of such letters as that of 27 October, 1777, in which inserted paragraphs are indicated, it can be seen that the Green Book contains drafts of his letters, from which he then made fair copies to send. However, the differences between the three letters to Percy held by the British Library and the drafts in Bowle's Green Book are minor.

There are other letters in these two volumes of the Bowle-Evans collection worthy of publication. Bowle's 1777-83 correspondence with another English Hispanist, John Dillon, would be a logical sequel to the present edition.[2]

Bowle and Percy

The letters reveal the methods and priorities of Bowle, the first scholarly editor of Don Quixote, and illuminate the insufficiently-known Spanish interests of Thomas Percy. The only preceding scholarship on Cervantes was biographical: the then-unpublished research of fray Martín Sarmiento,[3] Mayáns´ life of Cervantes, commissioned for the Don Quixote edition of Carteret (London, 1737-38),[4] and, during the period covered by these letters, the "Noticias para la vida de Miguel de Cervantes Saavedra" of Juan Antonio Pellicer.[5] Annotations of previous editions were insignificant, especially compared with Bowle's volume of annotations (volume 3 of his edition). With Percy and Bowle—and specifically in these letters—we are witness to the birth of the study of Don Quixote, central to the beginning of Hispanism.

Thomas Percy

While Bowle has been known to cervantistas since the publication of his edition in 1781, and his scholarly career has been the subject of two books,[6] the Hispanic interests of the famous and influential Percy are much less known. The importance of Spain and especially Cervantes for his scholarly career has not yet been realized.

   Although Bowle, in the published Letter to Dr.
Percy which presented his projected edition, called
Cervantes "our favourite writer," there has been no
way for scholars to verify that Bowle knew or was cor-
rectly presenting Percy´s opinion of Don Quixote, and
that statement was ignored.7 Percy´s Hispanism, in
fact, was virtually unknown until the donation of some
newly discovered papers to the Bodleian Library in
1932. Among them were proof sheets of an uncompleted
volume of poems translated from the Spanish, issued in
a limited edition by Oxford University Press the same
year. In the introduction to the Oxford edition there
were published letters in which Percy mentioned a proposed edition of Don Quixote and stated that "the
Spanish is a language I have long cultivated and Don
Quixote has always been my favourite Book." However,
the Oxford edition is itself a rarity, now rarer than
eighteenth-century editions of Percy´s Reliques of Ancient English Poetry. The only studies of Percy´s
Hispanism, prior to the recent discovery of these letters, were a short article in the Bulletin of Spanish
Studies, motivated by the Oxford edition, and a German
dissertation.8

   The present letters have been known through an
article and a book chapter,9 which, however, contained
only brief excerpts from them. Their publication do-
cuments beyond any doubt Percy´s love for Don Quixote
and his activities as collector of Spanish books. He
repeatedly calls Cervantes "our favourite author"
(letters of 24 October, 1767; 22 June, 1771; 24 March,
1774; 15 February, 1775; 3 February, 1777; 22 May,
1777; 15 July, 1781), and Spanish literature "my favourite Subject" (2 April, 1768). We see not only his
efforts to assemble a "Quixotic library,"10 but also
his plans for "an improved Translation with large
Notes & Illustrations: as well containing Criticisms
on the Spanish Phraseology of the Author, as large

Extracts from the old Romances by way of a Key to his Satire" (2 April, 1768).

Percy´s work was in time to be taken over by Bowle, whose activities were more specialized and who had, as Percy wrote (2 April, 1768), more leisure. From the letters we can determine fairly closely the chronology of the shift. Percy had need of his <u>Amadís</u> in 1769 (20 June, 1769), and on 11 January, 1772, referred to "our great Research." In April of that year he wrote that he collected "Quixotic" books "latterly as much for your use, as my own." (This is also the point at which Bowle began to keep copies of his letters.) By 2 June, 1772, work on <u>Don Quixote</u> was referred to as "your learned & ingenious Persuits." While Bowle on 30 January, 1773, courteously referred to "our present pursuits," and in 1774 wrote "be it yours in due time to give him an English Dress" (31 March, 1774), the last statement suggests already a project set aside. In 1775, writing to Bowle, it is "your reasearches" (15 February, 1775), and in 1778 Percy wrote, sadly, "I am only sorry that I must continue an idle Spectator of your curious Researches, without being able to advance them" (29 August, 1778).

The letters show how Percy, in contrast with Bowle, was interested in "Spanish Romances of Chivalry," a term which he was apparently the first to use. The role of Percy´s enormously influential <u>Reliques</u> in sparking the revival of interest in older and medieval literature ("romances") in England and Germany is well known. One can see, from all of this evidence, that Percy´s English literary antiquarianism was antedated by his interest in <u>Don Quixote</u>, "<u>always</u> [his] favourite book" (emphasis added), and by the "romances" of Spain, to which <u>Don Quixote</u> led him. One may well propose his Hispanism and Cervantism as not just a predecessor but a cause.[11]

John Bowle

The Reverend John Bowle (1725-1788) is the editor and publisher of the first scholarly edition of Don Quixote (1781), with the preparation of which the present letters in large part deal. He was the first to annotate the book, attempting to explain its numerous allusions; he was the initiator of textual study of the work, collating different editions and discovering that there were two 1605 editions of Part I; he was the first to prepare an index to the book and to take such a modest but useful step as numbering the lines of his edition (see letter of 28 July, 1780).

While Bowle´s approach to Don Quixote can be found in and deduced from his publications, these letters confirm and add background to it. His goal is to understand Don Quixote in a very literal sense: to know what its words and proverbs mean, to identify the places and books mentioned. Secondarily, Bowle wants to show that Cervantes is what he calls a "classical" author, meaning both that Cervantes is of the importance of the great Greek and Latin authors, and that, like them, he was possessed of great learning. While Bowle is apparently the first to refer to the irony of Don Quixote (letter of 31 March, 1774), such modern concerns as Cervantes´ literary theory or generic concepts were unknown to him. Nowhere in these letters is any other of Cervantes´ works mentioned.

To find information which would explain the text of Don Quixote, Bowle read through books mentioned in the text, a large number of other books potentially available to Cervantes, and some books Cervantes could not have known but which might offer relevant information. His considerable pains in searching for books are evident; as he wrote Percy (11 February, 1775; 25 March, 1776), some of them needed repeated readings, part drudgery and part exhilaration. His annotations, we find, were kept interleaved with a copy of the text.[12]

Not the least of the attractions of these letters are the glimpses they reveal of a past scholar´s life. Bowle´s years of research and pride and confidence in the results, his "astonishment as [his notes] arise out of a Chaos" (letter of 28 July, 1780), are still familiar experiences to many. Those were exciting times when one could bid at auction for a copy of Avellaneda and have <u>Tirante</u> <u>el</u> <u>Blanco</u> loaned, as long as it were safely packed up for its return, when one could make such discoveries as the varying text in the different editions of Juan de la Cuesta and the two editions of 1605. At the same time, Bowle lacked the most fundamental of tools. The few collections of Spanish books in England were in private hands. Supply of books from Spain was irregular and depended to a considerable extent on personal contacts. The only way to get a copy of a text which could not be purchased was to copy it out in longhand (or set it in type, also by hand). For bibliography he had only Nicolás Antonio, for dictionaries <u>Autoridades</u>, which he calls "the Madrid dictionary," and later Covarrubias´ <u>Tesoro</u>. There was no published history of Spanish literature; biographical information on Cervantes was, by today´s standards, very limited.

Bowle´s edition, as Cox has revealed, was not greeted with unanimous acclaim, and Bowle´s final years were somewhat embittered by controversy. However, with the passsage of time he has triumphed over his detractors. It is appropriate to conclude this discussion of Bowle by quoting some comments on his edition, the reprinting of which is highly desirable. George Ticknor said of it: "there are few books of so much real learning, and at the same time of so little pretension. ... It is, in fact, the true and safe foundation on which has been built much of what has since been done with success for the explanation and illustration of the <u>Don</u> <u>Quixote</u>."[13] According to

Julio Casares, Bowle's "famosas 'anotaciones', discutidas, mejoradas y con harta frecuencia saqueadas por quienes vinieron después, despiertan todavía admiración y pueden estudiarse con fruto."14

Agustín G. de Amezúa y Mayo has made the most substantial evaluation of Bowle's work: "En la empresa de comentar el Quijote [eran necesarios] tiempo, estudio y literaria probidad, dotes y circunstancias que, por fortuna para Cervantes, viéronse reunidas en un excelente varón, entusiasta por extremo de la incomparable novela, el reverendo doctor Juan Bowle, a quien puede reputarse por verdadero patriarca de los cervantistas y benemérito entre todos por la ejemplar obra que realizó. Para acometerla, pertrechóse primero de un gran número de libros antiguos castellanos, y dentro de ellos de los caballerescos; Bowle es, ciertamente, el primero que benefició esta cantera tan esencial para la recta inteligencia del Quijote;15 lee también los poemas heroicos italianos; maneja las colecciones de romances; repasa las crónicas y monografías históricas, y, por vez primera también, traza parcialmente el mapa de la picaresca española. Podrá haber cierta candorosidad en su comentario, tan justificada en un extranjero con su ingenua sintaxis; pero en general todas sus notas están concebidas y redactadas con gran discreción y excelente criterio, sin que nunca se aventure a dar paso alguno ni sentar afirmación que no tenga su arrimo en libros y autores dignos de toda fe. ... Bowle es el primero también que saca a Cervantes de su carácter de escritor puramente nacional. ... Obra, en suma, la de Bowle admirable y digna de loa por extremo; tanto más que, no contentándose con su solo comento, fue el primero también que formó un vocabulario cervantino y sacó el índice de los nombres propios contenidos en la inmortal novela. Y como si no fuera bastante, a él se deben asimismo los primeros cotejos de su texto, con la anotación de algunas variantes de las ediciones primitivas, nuevo aspecto de trabajo crítico y esbozo de secciones que con los

años tanta importancia alcanzarían en los estudios del
Qui_jote."16

This edition

The transcription of these letters has been no
trivial chore. They are multilingual and filled with
obscure proper names; many names and quotations use ob-
solete spellings or are simply misspelled. (There are
too many of these to add "sic" after each one.) It is
often difficult to tell capital from small letters and
to identify the punctuation marks used. Furthermore,
while the letters of Percy are relatively clearly written, most of those of Bowle survive in drafts, written
for his eyes only, in a small and difficult hand, and
sometimes with very inconsistent spelling.17 Adding to
the editor's problems is the fact that most of the materials are located in South Africa, and of necessity I
have worked exclusively from copies. All the same, a
number of errors found in the previously published excerpts have been eliminated.

Some explanatory notes on the persons and books
mentioned in the letters will be found in the Index.

Considering the interests of projected readers, my
own interests and skills, and the nature of this
series, the correspondence has been abbreviated by some
20% by the deletion of material of no Hispanic interest, dealing primarily with British antiquities. Omis-
sions are marked with ellipses in the text. In a few
instances it was impractical to delete a small item,
and from these an idea of the deletions may be obtained.

In general I have tried to follow the spelling and
punctuation of the originals, although for typo-
graphical reasons no superscript letters have been

used. To avoid confusion between my own editorial brackets and those of Bowle himself, I have used the brace { } to represent Bowle's brackets.

Some very minor editorial alterations have been tacitly made. Most cancelled words are illegible, at least on the copies, but I have not recorded those which are legible, such as the words "in England" cancelled preceding "in your neighbourhood" in Percy's letter of 12 March, 1767. The abbreviation ye is transcribed as "the," and Percy's occasional dittography of words has been removed.

Acknowledgements

This edition would not exist were it not for the assistance and encouragement of R. Merritt Cox and Bert Davis. Both have been most generous in sharing materials and advice with me. Bert Davis kindly checked my transcriptions of all the letters of Percy, and has also elucidated a number of allusions within them. For many suggestions and identifications I am indebted to W. Hunter.

I would also like to thank the University of Cape Town Library for authorizing this publication.

Notes

1. The Bowle-Evans Collection in the University of Cape Town Library (Rondebosch, 1958) (mimeographed). I am indebted to R. Merritt Cox for a copy.

2. The contents of the Epistolarium and the Green Book are reviewed chronologically by R. Merritt Cox, An English "Ilustrado": The Reverend John Bowle (Bern: Peter Lang, 1977), Chapters IV and V.

John Dillon was author of Travels in Spain, with a View to Illustrate the Natural History and Physical Geography of that Kingdom (London, 1780), and of the anonymous Letters from an English Traveller in Spain, in 1778, on the Origin and Progress of Poetry in that Kingdom; with Occasional Reflections on Manners and Customs, and Illustrations of the Romance of Don Quixote. Adorned with portraits of the Most Eminent Poets (London, 1781). On Dillon, see Otis H. Green, "Sir John Talbot Dillon and his Letters on Spanish Literature (1778)," HR, 41 (1973), 253-60; and Cox, An English "Ilustrado," p. 108, n. 7, and p. 111, n. 4.

3. Author of the Noticia de la verdadera patria (Alcalá) de él [sic] Miguel de Cervantes, first published in Barcelona in 1898, and numerous other scholarly works which were not published in his lifetime and in some cases are still unpublished. This Noticia includes the "Disertación sobre el Amadís de Gaula" discussed by Barton Sholod, "Fray Martín Sarmiento, Amadís de Gaula and the Spanish Chivalric ´Genre´," in Studies in Honor of Mario A. Pei, University of North Carolina Studies in Romance Languages and Literatures, 114 (Chapel Hill: University of North Carolina Press, 1972), pp. 183-99.

4. The only exception to this would be the Cervantine scholarship of Bodmer in Germany. On it, and Bodmer´s role in initiating modern interest in medieval German

literature, see the Appendix to my A Study of "Don Quixote" (Newark, Delaware: Juan de la Cuesta, 1987). On Lord Carteret's edition, a study of which is a desideratum, see the edition of Mayáns' Vida by Antonio Mestre, Clásicos Castellanos, 172 (Madrid: Espasa-Calpe, 1972); a review essay by Francisco Brines was published in Cuadernos Hispanoamericanos, No. 297 (March, 1975), 582-98.

5. Published in the author's Ensayo de una Biblioteca de traductores españoles (Madrid, 1778).

6. R. Merritt Cox, An English "Ilustrado," already cited, and The Rev. John Bowle. The Genesis of Cervantean Criticism, University of North Carolina Studies in the Romance Languages and Literatures, 99 (Chapel Hill: University of North Carolina Press, 1971).

7. See letter No. 36, below.

8. A. Watkin-Jones, "A Pioneer Hispanist: Thomas Percy," Bulletin of Spanish Studies, 14 (1937), 3-9; Gisela Beutler, Thomas Percy's spanische Studien, ein Beitrag zum Bild Spaniens in England in der zweiten Hälfte des 18. Jahrhunderts (Bonn, 1957).

9. R. Merritt Cox, An English "Ilustrado," Chapter IV; without knowledge of Cox's book, Cleanth Brooks, "Thomas Percy, Don Quixote, and Don Bowle," in Evidence in Literary Scholarship. Essays in Memory of James Marshall Osborn, ed. René Wellek and Alvaro Ribeiro (Oxford: Clarendon Press, 1979), pp. 247-61.

10. Percy's "Quixotic Library" is reconstructed and annotated by Beutler, pp. 367-400. The books in Don Quixote's library cannot be assembled by purchase, as some of them are too rare. (Another partial attempt was made in the nineteenth century by the Marqués de Salamanca; see Isidro Bonsoms y Sicart, Discursos leídos en la Real Academia de Buenas Letras de Barce-

lona en la recepción pública de D. Isidro Bonsoms y Sicart [Barcelona, 1907], and Homero Serís, "La reaparición del Tirant lo Blanch de Barcelona de 1497," in Homenaje a Menéndez Pidal [Madrid: Hernando, 1925], III, 57-76.) I have proposed, in "Did Cervantes Have a Library?," Hispanic Studies in Honor of Alan D. Deyermond. A North American Tribute (Madison: Hispanic Seminary of Medieval Studies, 1986), pp. 93-106, that Don Quixote's library is to be identified with that of Cervantes, and have offered a hypothetical reconstruction of the latter, with the suggestion that it be recreated on microfilm or some similar medium, in "La biblioteca de Cervantes," Studia in Honorem Prof. M. de Riquer, II (Barcelona: Quaderns Crema, in press).

11. On this, see my A Study of "Don Quixote," Appendix.

12. This copy is now in the library of the Hispanic Society of America. See Cox, The Rev. John Bowle, p. 52.

13. History of Spanish Literature, 6th American edition, 3 vols (Boston: Houghton, Mifflin, 1891), III, *437.

14. "Las tres edades del Quijote," BRAE, 27 (1948), 43-60, at pp. 43-44.

15. As Armando Cotarelo Valledor pointed out in El "Quijote" académico (Madrid: Instituto de España, 1948), pp. 14-15, the Spanish Academy decided, in preparing its recently-reprinted edition of 1780, that there was no need for such chivalric annotations.

16. Agustín G. de Amezúa, "Epílogo sobre esta edición crítica de El ingenioso hidalgo, dispuesta por Don Francisco Rodríguez Marín," in Rodríguez Marín's "nueva edición crítica," VIII (Madrid: Atlas, 1948), 273-301, at pp. 276-77. Amezúa continues with an attack

on his countrymen: "Mas, a pesar de la manifiesta bondad de esta edición de El ingenioso hidalgo, tan doctamente ilustrada por el doctor Bowle, ... recibióse en España con notoria indiferencia, ya que no pasaron de cinco las suscripciones que logró en nuestra patria, desdén realmente lamentable, y al que no cabe dar otra excusa o explicación sino la de que las abundantes ediciones suyas que por entonces se hacían entre nosotros, entre ellas la primera y espléndida de la Real Academia Española, parecían convertir en innecesarias las venidas de afuera. Pero, con todo eso, la iniciativa del doctor Bowle tenía que abochornar a los eruditos indígenas, por ser un extranjero quien se anticipaba a ilustrar nuestro libro más nacional, declarando implícitamente con ello su incapacidad para realizar otro tanto" (pp. 277-78).

17. For example, in Bowle's letter of 12 November, 1778, in his letterbook the name of the second son of the Duke of Northumberland is given as "Algernon Piercy," while in the letter sent, now in the British Library, it is "Algernoon Percy"; I have given it in the correct form, Algernon Percy.

Works Cited

Amezúa, Agustín G. de, "Epílogo sobre esta edición crítica de El ingenioso hidalgo, dispuesta por Don Francisco Rodríguez Marín," in Rodríguez Marín's "nueva edición crítica," VIII (Madrid: Atlas, 1948), 273-301.

Beutler, Gisela, Thomas Percy's spanische Studien, ein Beitrag zum Bild Spaniens in England in der zweiten Hälfte des 18. Jahrhunderts. Bonn, 1957.

Bonsoms y Sicart, Isidro, Discursos leídos en la Real Academia de Buenas Letras de Barcelona en la recepción pública de D. Isidro Bonsoms y Sicart. Barcelona, 1907.

Bowle, John, "Remarks on the Word 'Romance'," Archaeologia, 5 (1779), 267-71.

--------, A Letter to the Reverend Dr. Percy, concerning a New and Classical Edition of "Historia del valeroso cavallero Don Quixote de la Mancha." London, 1777.

--------, ed., Historia del famoso cavallero, Don Quixote de la Mancha. Salisbury, 1781; rpt. London, 1781. (Though I have seen it, unfortunately I have not been able to use a copy of this rare edition during the editing of these letters; the annotations, though not the preliminary material, are reproduced in Cox´s dissertation.)

--------, Review of the Real Academia edition of <u>Don</u> <u>Quixote</u>, <u>Gentleman´s</u> <u>Magazine</u>, 53 (1783), 812-13.

--------, Letters to the Editor, <u>Gentleman´s</u> <u>Magazine</u>, 51 (1781), 22-24 (on Pellicer´s "Noticias para la vida de Miguel de Cervantes Saavedra," in his <u>Ensayo</u> <u>de</u> <u>una</u> <u>biblioteca</u> <u>de</u> <u>traductores</u> <u>españoles</u>); 54 (1784), 565-66; 55 (1785), 414.

Brooks, Cleanth, "Thomas Percy, <u>Don</u> <u>Quixote</u>, and Don Bowle," in <u>Evidence</u> <u>in</u> <u>Literary</u> <u>Scholarship.</u> <u>Essays</u> <u>in</u> <u>Memory</u> <u>of</u> <u>James</u> <u>Marshall</u> <u>Osborn</u>, ed. René Wellek and Alvaro Ribeiro (Oxford: Clarendon Press, 1979), pp. 247-61.

Bryant, Shasta M., <u>The</u> <u>Spanish</u> <u>Ballad</u> <u>in</u> <u>English</u>. Lexington: University Press of Kentucky, 1973.

Casares, Julio, "Las tres edades del <u>Quijote</u>," <u>BRAE</u>, 27 (1948), 43-60.

Cox, R. Merritt, "Cervantes and Three <u>Ilustrados</u>: Mayáns, Sarmiento, and Bowle," in <u>Studies</u> <u>in</u> <u>the</u> <u>Spanish</u> <u>Golden</u> <u>Age:</u> <u>Cervantes</u> <u>and</u> <u>Lope</u> <u>de</u> <u>Vega</u> (Miami: Universal, 1978), pp. 12-20.

--------, <u>An</u> <u>English</u> <u>"Ilustrado":</u> <u>The</u> <u>Reverend</u> <u>John</u> <u>Bowle</u>. Bern, Frankfurt am Main, Las Vegas: Peter Lang, 1977.

--------, "The Library of the Reverend John Bowle: Revelations in English Hispanism," in <u>Studies</u> <u>in</u> <u>Honor</u> <u>of</u> <u>Gerald</u> <u>E.</u> <u>Wade</u> (Madrid: José Porrúa Turanzas, 1979), pp. 23-34.

--------, "The Rev. John Bowle: First Editor of <u>Don</u> <u>Quixote</u>." Diss. Wisconsin, 1967. (Includes Bowle´s annotations, though keyed to Bowle´s pages and lines rather than to chapters. Useful, but no substitute for a reprint. The remainder of the dissertation was published as the book listed below.)

--------, "The Rev. John Bowle: The First Editor of Don Quixote," Studies in Philology, 67 (1970), 103-15.

--------, The Rev. John Bowle. The Genesis of Cervantean Criticism. University of North Carolina Studies in the Romance Languages and Literatures, 99. Chapel Hill: University of North Carolina Press, 1971.

Davis, Bertram H., Thomas Percy. Boston: Twayne, 1981.

Eisenberg, Daniel, "La biblioteca de Cervantes," in Studia in Honorem Prof. M. de Riquer, II (Barcelona: Quaderns Crema, in press).

--------, "Did Cervantes Have a Library?," in Hispanic Studies in Honor of Alan D. Deyermond. A North American Tribute (Madison: Hispanic Seminary of Medieval Studies, 1986), pp. 93-106,

--------, A Study of "Don Quixote." Newark, Delaware: Juan de la Cuesta, 1987. (Appendix: "The Influence of Don Quixote on the Romantic Movement.")

Immelman, R. F. M., The Bowle-Evans Collection in the University of Cape Town Library. Rondebosch, 1958. (Mimeographed.)

Mayáns y Siscar, Gregorio, Vida de Miguel de Cervantes Saavedra. First published in 1737. Ed. with introduction by Antonio Mestre. Clásicos Castellanos, 172. Madrid: Espasa-Calpe, 1972. Review essay by Francisco Brines, Cuadernos Hispanoamericanos, No. 297 (March, 1975), 582-98.

Pellicer, Juan Antonio, Ensayo de una Biblioteca de traductores españoles. Madrid, 1778. See supra, Bowle, Letters to the Editor, for his comments on this work.

Percy, Thomas, Ancient Songs Chiefly on Moorish Subjects Translated from the Spanish, ed. David Nichol Smith. London: Oxford University Press, 1932.

Serís, Homero, "La reaparición del Tirant lo Blanch de Barcelona de 1497," in Homenaje a Menéndez Pidal (Madrid: Hernando, 1925), III, 57-76.

Smith, Gilbert, "El cervantismo en las polémicas literarias del siglo XVIII," in Cervantes. Su obra y su mundo. Actas del I Congreso Internacional sobre Cervantes (Madrid: Edi-6, 1981), pp. 1031-35.

The Thomas Percy Collection [Catalogue]. [Tallahassee]: Strozier Library, Florida State University, 1985.

Ticknor, George, History of Spanish Literature. 6th American edition. 3 vols. Boston: Houghton, Mifflin, 1891.

Watkin-Jones, A., "A Pioneer Hispanist: Thomas Percy," Bulletin of Spanish Studies, 14 (1937), 3-9.

PERCY——BOWLE

CERVANTINE CORRESPONDENCE

Northumberland House, Charing Cross
Feb. 11. 1767.

Sir,

Calling in at Mr. [Andrew] Jackson's Shop this
morning, he tells me You were so good as to speak of
some curious particulars you had, or could direct me
to, relating to the subject of the Old Minstrels: I
should be much obliged to you, Sir, if you would do me
the favour to communicate the same to me, or inform
me, where I could have recourse to them. As a New
Edit. of the Old Reliques is coming out, any Information for improving that little Work wd. be thankfully
accepted: and a Copy of the Book, when published, will
be the least Acknowledgmt. you will be intitled to
from

Sir

Your most humble Servant

Thos. Percy

Northumberland House, Mar. 12. 1767.

Sir,

I recd. the very obliging favour of your Letter,
and hope it will be the fore-runner of many others
equally curious and entertaining: I shall not fail to
profit by the Hints you are so good as to impart to
me, for improving this new Edition of the Ancient
Poems; a Copy of which will solicit your acceptance.
[...]

Inclosed I send a very full Catalogue of Don Quixote's Library [not found]: You will at once see what
I have; and what I want. --The latter articles the
more easily to catch your eye are denoted by an Aster-
isk (*). --Such as I want extremely by two asterisks
(**). --One of them, viz. El virdadero Succeso de la
batalla de Roncesvalles was not long since in your
neighbourhood, & perhaps may be unnoticed in some
booksellers shop in Salisbury still: --I shd. be glad
to get it at any Rate. --I must also implore your
Assistance, as I do that of every Man of Letters, towards compleating my Quixotic Library: I only accumu-
late them for the Public Benefit, and this emboldens
me to solicit every one's help. You are so curious in
your Researches that I flatter myself with great Success by your kind Assistance, in concurrence with my
own constant, unremitted inquiries. --There are many
illustrations, inlargements &c of my Catalogue &c may
be found in Mayans y Siscar's Life of Cervantes, & to
that work I refer you for further Particulars. [...]

Your most obedient Servant

Thos. Percy

Northumberland House. April 2d. 1767.

Dear Sir,

I am indebted to you so much for your kind Letter & most obliging Present of the books, that I cannot defer paying my grateful Acknowledgments, tho´ I am obliged to write this Evening without a Frank; which I hope you will pardon. --I am extremely sorry for the Indisposition you have suffered: Nor have I been free from Illness myself, tho´ now, (thank God) I am perfectly restored. I have made so much Use of the curious Hints you have imparted to me on the Subjects of Minstrelsy & Dramatic History, that you must not be surprized if you see your name mentioned in My Preface. [...]

Your Nimphas de Henares & Possevino make a very important Figure in my Libreria Quixotesca: which I flatter myself is going to receive some further Accessions: for an ingenious Friend is going to make the Tour of Flanders & has promised to inquire at all the Shops in Brucelas, Amberes and all those Towns, which were so long Part of the Spanish Monarchy & where so many Spanish Books were printed & published. Whatever is the Result of his Research, you may expect to be early acquainted with it: For as you are so good as to interest yourself in the Increase of my Collection, the least return I can make is to give you continual Accounts of my Success: tho´ indeed every book in it is as intirely at your Service, as if it were in your Own Library & I cannot enjoy a greater pleasure than to submit them to so compleat a Judge of their Use. --I hope soon to be able to present you with my New Edit. of the Ancient Reliques wch. are almost printed off. [...]

Your very faithful Servant

Thos. Percy

PS I hope you will collect together any Hints for illustrating Shakespeare that have occurred to you, for
the benefit of my frie[n]d Mr. [George] Steevens.

4

Northumbd. House Jun. 25. [1767]

Dear Sir,

Do me the favour to inform me how I can convey to
you my New Edition of Old Poetry, which you will find
much inriched with curious particulars imparted to me
by yourself. I write in haste, fearful lest we shd.
leave town before I can have your Answer. The Duke
has the Gout in his hands wch. prevents him from
franking my Letter, otherwise you shd. not pay postage
for this shabby Scrawl. I am

Dear Sir

Your most faithful Servant

Tho. Percy

Northumbd. House July. 13. 1767.

Dear Sir,

    I recd. the favour of your obliging Letter &
agreeably to your Directions sent the Books to Mr.
Horsefields, in Ludgate Street &c. I hope by this
time they are got safe to Salisbury. ---You tell me
you have lately met with some farther Particulars relating to four of my late Subjects of Disquisition,
which you cd. have communicated to me, but that they
occurred too late: I shd. be very glad <u>yet</u> to know
what they are: for tho My Book can´t profit by them,
the Editor may; and while I have the subject still
fresh in my mind any curious Particulars will be extremely satisfactory & amusing.

    I am much obliged to you for your kind attention
to my Quixotic Researches, & hope your obliging Labours in my Favour will meet with Success.

    I am just setting out with this family for the
North, & shd. be glad to receive any epistolary Favours under Cover to his Grace the Duke of Northumbd.
at Alnwick Castle in Northumberld.

    I am, Dear Sir

Your very faithful humble Servant

Tho. Percy

Northumberland House. Oct. 24. 1767.

Dear Sir,

I certainly should not have let your obliging Letter of Aug. 27. have remained so long unacknowledged had not my attention been wholly turned aside from literary persuits, and the other agreeable subjects, you discuss in your Letter, by a great variety of avocations that have wholly engrossed me for these 2 months past: I have been much a traveller within this period, as you will infer from the Distance of my present situation from that to which you addressed your last Letter: This & many other matters of private Concernmt. will, I trust, both account, and apologize to you for my silence.

I shall be extremely glad to see the passages you mention in the Code of Spanish Laws, which you think are alluded to in the writings of Cervantes, & which will justify you in dissenting from Don Gregorio de Siscar, in some particulars respecting our favourite author. --These or any other curious Subjects of your Disquisition I shall ever be glad to see: nor can you do me a more acceptable favour than by communicating them to me at all times without ceremony, or formal Introduction.

I am much obliged to you for being so good as to think of me, and to endeavour, thus constantly as you do, to assist me in compleating my Libreria Quixotesca: I have given Lists of the Books I want to many Friends & Acquaintance now upon their Travels in France & Italy: but expect so much from none of them as from an English Merchant, long resident in Spain, & who returns thither this present autumn: He has taken a List of my Libri Desiderati; which he has promised to procure for me. And if there are any others, which you would wish to procure for yourself: let me have their titles and I will transmit them to him.

I am obliged to you for the curious hints you impart to me on the subject of the <u>Minstrels</u> & shall not fail to profit by your reference to Crescembeni [sic; ´Crescimbeni´], & by the other Books you mention in your Letter. --I shd. be glad if you would give me a more particular account of the <u>Scalping</u> practiced in France & England, which you mention.

I have been lately endeavouring to get Copies of the old Metrical Romances, enumerated in the 3d. Vol. of my Book: Many of my friends having importuned very strongly that a Collection of them mt. be published.

I have also been urging old Jackson to read over all the old English Versions of Amadis, Esplandian, and the other Spanish Romances of Chivalry: with a particular View to Don Quixote: which I have also persuaded him to read in the old English Version of Shelton. --Till I can undertake this sort of work, myself, in form, I am glad to excite all my acquaintance to be doing somewhat towards it before hand.

I am, with real regard, Dear Sir

Your very obliged & faithful servant

Thos. Percy.

Northumberland House. Jany. 21. [1768]

Dear Sir,

I shd. not have let so obliging a Letter as yours of Novr. 17th. have remained so long unacknowledged, had it not arrived here at a time when I was absent from London on a long Journey; which was attended with much consequent business that took me off from all literary persuits.

I am truly thankful for the many interesting particulars of curious Research with which your Letter abounds. I am astonished at your extent of knowledge in relation to Spanish and other Antiquities. I doubt whether there is any Man now in Spain, Who knows so much of the literary and genealogical History of that Nation, as yourself. I shall very gratefully avail myself of your discoveries, and am never so happy as when you communicate to me all such anecdotes as fall in your way.

I have not yet heard from Spain on the subject of my Book-Commissions: but whenever I do, and have an opportunity of writing thither again, I will not forget to insert the several articles you recommend to me in your last as what you cd. wish to have procured for you.

I have repeatedly inquired at Mr. Vaillants for the Books you commissioned him to import for you: and yesterday he told me that he expected soon a large Bale of Spanish Books: of which he promised to favour me with the earliest Account, as soon they arrived. This, as soon as I receive it, I shall not fail to transmit to you. --I have lately had the good fortune to make one or two important additions to my Quixotic

Library viz. The Carolea in folio, mentioned in the Survey of the Curate & the Barber: and Una Selva de Romances containing not only the Ballad of Don Gayferos & Melesendra [II, 26]: but the whole story of the Marques de Mantua, which is so much alluded to in the Account of Don Quixote´s first Sally [I, 5].

I hope this approaching Spring will bring you to London, that I may shew you many literary Curiosities wch. I have picked up since you were here last. In the mean time I hope you will continue to favour me with your obliging Letters repleat with curious Articles of Information which will ever be gratefully acknowledged

by Dear Sir

Your most obedient & faithful Servant

Thos. Percy

Do you know anything of the merit of the following Books? viz
Principios del Reyno de Portugal [by Antonio Páez
    Viegas, 1641]
Dialogos de varia Hi[s]toria de Pedro de Mariz
Obras de Juan de Tarsis
Ramilla [sic; ´Ramillo´] o Guirnalda de Discursos
    politicos & ethicos [by Juan Lambrechsts, 1656]
Vida y accoens [sic; ´acçoens´] del Rey Don Juan [by
    Fernâo de Menezes, 1677]
Obras varias de Geronimo de Cancer y Velasco
Conseios politicos y morales de Don Rodrigo Diaz
As Obras do Dautor [sic] Fran[cisc]o. De Saa de Mi-
    randa
Ocios del Conde de Rebellido [sic; ´Rebolledo´]

This List was sent me by a Country Book-Seller

Northmbd. House. Apr. 2d. 1768

Dear Sir,

   Your Letters are always so replete with curious &
entertaining Information, on my favourite Subject of
Spanish Literature, &c that nothing can be more wel-
come to me than an Epistolary Favour from you. Your
last shd. have been acknowledged sooner but for the
Election Riots, which have created so much disturbance
here & left no Leisure for any literary or amusing
Subject. I have at length however snatched up the Pen
to tell you that I have got a most valuable addition
to my Stock of Quixotic Books; in a little old Volume
of <u>Canciones</u> y <u>Romances</u>, lately acquired, In which I
find the Old Song (wch. I have so long sought after)
of the Hist. of the <u>Marques</u> <u>of</u> <u>Mantua</u>, so particularly
referred to in many places of Don Quixote [I, 5]:
Here I find the lines quoted by the Knight, when he
fancied himself El herido cavallero del Bosque [I, 5].
viz

             Donde estas señora mia
             Que no te duele mi male &c &c
Here is also the famous Vow, which the Marques made to
revenge the Death of his Nephew, & which the Knight of
La Mancha imitates [I, 10] viz

     Juro por Dios verdadero
     y por Scta Maria su madre
     Y al Sancto Sacramento
     Que aqui suelen celebrare   Do you recollect in
     De nunca peynar mis canas   what passages of Don
     Ni las barbas me tocare   Quixote any refer-
     De no vestir otras ropas   ence is made to the
     Ni renovar mi calçare   Marquis of Mantua.
     De entrar en un poblado   If you do, please to
     Ni las armas me quitare   send me a List of
     Sino fuere por un hora   them.

Para mi cuerpo limpiare
De no comer en manteles
Ni a mesa me assentare
Hasta matar a Don Carloto
O morir en la demanda &c. &c.

The same book also contains a more authentic Copy than I had before, of Don Gayferos y Melisendra. --I want, now, scarce any old Spanish Ballad But the Verdadero Suceso de la Batalla de Roncesvalles: --And even on this I have got a large Poem in 35 Cantos, written by Nicolas Espinosa, as a 2d. Part to Urrea´s Translation of Orlando Furioso. The title is La segunda Parte de Orlando, Con el verdadero Sucesso de la Famosa Batalla de Roncesvalles, fin y muerte de los doze Pares de Francia &c por Nicolas Espinosa &c Anvers. 1556 4to. --I have also picked up a great many pieces of Lope de Vega. particularly his Philomena. 4to His Hermosura de Angelica in 20 cantos. His Sonetos and his Dragontea in 10 Cantos (a poem on the Death of Sr. Francis Drake.) I wish you could have taken a trip to Town that I might have show[n] them to you & many other things, you wd. enjoy more than me. I rejoice at what you tell me of your Copiosissimo Indice pray persevere in it: I shall sometime attempt, if not a new edition, of the Original: yet an improved Translation with large Notes & Illustrations: as well containing Criticisms on the Spanish Phraseology of the Author, as large Extracts from the old Romances by way of a Key to his Satire. I wish there fore you wd. note down, as you read him, all our authors Allusions, References to, Quotations of, & accidental or particular Mention of any of the Old Books of Chivalry. After that I wish you would read over some of my Old Books of Chivalry & Romance, to see what illustration they wd. afford Cervantes. You have leisure & retirement: I have neither in my present situation; & it will probably be some years before I attain either. Such assistance as this would be, would encourage me & enable me to bring my Scheme to a much earlier conclu-

sion than I shall ever be able to do otherwise. As I have Duplicates of some of the Romances, you could be reading them in the Country, while I was occasionally examining the Passages, you referred me to, here in Town. --Pray think of this Proposal & oblige me with your Sentiments upon it.
--You shd. begin with the Spanish <u>Amadis</u> <u>de</u> <u>Gaula.</u> <u>en</u> <u>4</u> <u>Libros</u> --then proceed to <u>Amadis</u> <u>de</u> <u>grecia</u>, &c and I would supply you with the Books.

I am, Dear Sir,   Very Truly

Your most faithful Servant

T. Percy

P.S. I am going out of Town for about 3 weeks: let me find a Letter from you at my return. Pray have you seen <u>La</u> <u>vie</u> <u>de</u> <u>Petrarque</u> [by Abbé de Sade, 1764-76] en 3 Tomes. 4to in French newly published: a most curious book: Throwing prodigious light on the origin of Italian &c Poetry, and illustrating all the old Italian Poets. --It is now to be sold in London. --Pray shall I send you Ozells version of Mayans y Siscar´s Life of Cervantes. I can buy one separate for 1-6d in quarto: interleave it & fill it with Notes & Improvements. --I called yesterday at Vaillants: But no Spanish Books were arrived or expected soon.

Northumbd. House Oct. 20. 1768

Dear Sir,

I recd. your billet: you mt. well think I had forgot you: but that was not the case: Soon after I wrote to you in the Summer, I was hurried away in to the North, before I had time to send you the inter-leaved Life of Cervantes, wch. I promised you: You shall soon have it now; but previously let me beg a Line: A Gentn. of my Acquaintance [Rev. Lewis Dutens] is going to spend the Winter in Spain: He sets out in 8 or 10 days & will be back in the Spring. He hath offered to bring me any Spanish Books I want: Send me therefore a List of any you wd. wish to buy & he shall buy them along with those of

Dear Sir

Your faithful Servant

Thos. Percy

PS I shall be glad to receive (what I hardly deserve on acct. of my Silence) a long Letter full of Spanish & Italian Literature.

Northumbd. House Nov. 10. 1768

Dear Sir,

I have sent your List into Spain as you desired: I am now to inform you that there is in Osborne´s New Catalogue a large thin folio MS. containing the Pedigrees of most if not all of the Spanish Nobility charged <u>one</u> <u>Guinea</u>: If you would wish to have it, let me know by a <u>Line</u> & I will secure it for you: Who am (in great haste)

Dear Sir,

Your faithful Servant

Thos. Percy

Northumbd. House June 20. 1769

Dear Sir,

I hope you got well home & have continued so. I trouble you with a Line to beg the favour of you to return me (by the first Coach so that I may receive it before Saturday night, or then at farthest) the 2 vols. of <u>Amadis</u> <u>de</u> <u>Gaula</u> <u>Español</u> 12mo. and in return I will lend you my folio Edition, as soon as I am apprized that you are at leisure to begin to read it. I am

Dear Sir

Your faithful Servant

Thos. Percy

12

Alnwick Castle in Northumberland
Aug. 13. 1769.

Dear Sir,

I recd. your letter & the <u>Amadis</u>, which you returned me: I shall procure you the use of it again,
when you are ready to enter upon a Course of that sort
of reading in Earnest: In the mean time <u>Amadis de
Grecia</u> may perhaps be not improperly perused, for I
presume these sort of Legendary Narratives are little
consequential. I have the pleasure to inform you that
I have at last got Tirante el blanco in Spanish: it is
now at Paris, waiting to be sent me. --Pray have you
seen Kelly's New Translation of Don Quixote published
in weekly Numbers: if you have send me your opinion of
it, as it has not yet reached

Dear Sir

Your most obedient servant

Thomas Percy

PS Pray how are your Studies directed at present?
have you compleated your Index of Phrases? --Direct
to me under Cover To his Grace the Duke of Nd. at this
Castle as above.

17

Wen´sday Morng. 30th. Jany. [1771]

Dr. Percy´s Compliments to Mr. Bowle. He fears he shall be engaged till near two o´clock, but from that time to four he shall be happy to see him not only to-day, but every day he stays in Town.

14

Northumberland House 3 April 1771

Dear Sir,

You will, I trust, pardon my long Silence, when I inform you that I did not neglect your Commission at Baker´s Auction: the following articles I was fortunate enough to secure for you, & I shall have great pleasure in delivering them to you, when you come to Town, which I hope will be soon. viz.

Sale of Mr. [Philip Carteret] Webb´s Books

```
                                  s  d
8vo.  1085 ---------cost---  1:6
4to.  1339 ----------------  2:0
      1516 ---------------- 10:6
8vo.  1776 ----------------  3:0
                            ─────
                            17:0
```

All the other Articles were bought out of our hands. Tho´ the Multiplicity of the Duke´s business often makes me a dilatory Correspondent, I shall never ne-glect any Commands that you will intrust to

Dear Sir

Your very faithful Servant

Thos. Percy

PS There has been a sale of curious Books at Paterson´s but I never could get time once to attend it.

15

Northumberland House, June 22d. 1771

Dear Sir,

[...] --I hope you have enjoyed good health ever since I had the pleasure of seeing you in Town, and that you continue your persuits for the illustration of our favourite Author. I have lately been indulged with the Loan of a very curious old French Romance, wch. is the Old History of the <u>San Graal</u>: I wish I could see you in Town, before I return it to its owner, because I think you wd. find many curious old legends in it, alluded to by Cervantes: Particularly I think it is very likely to contain the <u>Fable of King Arthur´s</u> being changed into a Crow [I, 13], &c. &c. &c. --I am however to have the book a Twelve Month: & it shall go hard but you shall see it. --Baretti is returned to England and has brought with him, not only the first Volume (in Print) of <u>La Historia de Fray Gerundio</u>, with a View of republishing it: but he has also got the original MS. of the 2d. Volume, never yet published, which the author has committed to his Care, in order to have it printed. This will be a great Acquisition to our Spanish library-- The Author [Is-

1a] is a Spanish Jesuit, who has been banished into
Italy, with the rest of that unfortunate Order: and
luckily <u>Baretti</u> has Found him in his obscure retreat,
and will be a means of saving this fine Original Work
from Oblivion & Extinction.   --Baretti proposes to
give the whole work, in 2 handsome 4to. Volumes, by a
subscription of 2 Guineas. Adieu! Dear Sir, & favour
with a Speedy Answer

Your faithful Servant

Tho. Percy

16

11th. Jany. 1772

Dear Sir,

     You expressed a wish to have a Copy of this Sec-
tion of the Hermitage Chapel at Warworth in Northumbd.
Happily I have fo[und] one, wch. I have inclose & am

Dear Sir

Most Faithfully Yours

Thos. Percy

PS When I shall be favoured with an Account of your
Proceedings in our great Research &c. I am always
happy to hear from you. Do write to me a long Letter.

Idmestone Jany. 20. 1772

Rev. dr. Percy
under Cover to the
Duke of Northumberland
London

Dear Sir

I am much obliged to you for the favour of your
last Letter, & for the contents of it. I Labour in-
cessantly on the manuscript of my Index, which were I
not fortifyd with uncommon perseverance I should have
long ago deserted. I hope in due time to find the
Utile cum dulci in it. I shall not at present enlarge
on this topick, as I hope you will be able to devote
one Hour seriously to peruse what may finally appear
necessary towards making publick the design of a new
Edition which most certainly cannot be done in any
hurry. I have somewhat to say of the first Edition, &
of the Text of Lord Carterets, but this will come more
pertinently hereafter. I hope to be in London the
middle of next week. Many Years of Health & Happiness
attend you. I am, Sir, Your much obliged Humble Servant.

John Bowle

Northumbd. House. April. 6. 1772

Dear Sir,

I have recd. your List, relative to Beighton´s Sale, & shall purposely abstain from every book in it, tho´ some of them I had marked to bid for, except One Which you wd. very much oblige me, by resigning to me, especially as you shall have the intire use of it, at all times as much as myself, and it is so necessary to my Quixotic Library (which I have bought, latterly as much for your use, as my own) that it is defective without it; I mean Avellaneda´s Spurious Quixote: I mean to go higher than a Guinea; but hope, I shall not have you for my opponent, if it shd. be knocked down at less. --I therefore intreat the favour of you, either to withdraw you[r] Commission as to that Book, or, if you please, I will abstain from bidding & trust to your Commission. --Please to favour me with a Line, & let me know whether you have not got my Felix-marte de Yrcania, along with the others. [...]

I am   Dear Sir   Yours Sincerely

Thomas Percy

Idmiston. May 8. 72.

To Dr. Percy
under cover to Duke of Northumberland.
Lond.

Dear Sir.

As the letter with which you last favoured me did not arrive soon enough for any notice respecting my commissions, in every material one of which I have failed, I have taken my own time to answer yours. [...]

I shall be sorry if my Curiosity has been prejudicial to our mutual inquiries: & will therefore hope for the best & that Avellanada [sic] is where he should be in your possession: with this view give me leave to Invert a passage of Cervantes P.2.C.61. Bien sea venido, digo no el verdadero, el legal, y el fiel don Quixote de La Mancha que nos descrivio Cide Hamete Benengeli flor de los Historiadores, sino el falso, el ficticio, y el apocrifo que en falsas Historias nos han mostrado: if this should not be the case we must wait the event of Leacroft's Commission. Felix marte, alias Florismarte de Hircania stands unmolested with his two Brother Knights del Febo, & Oliva. Tirante is at a proper distance all well & kiss your hands. I hope to have the pleasure of a short conversation with you if I shall have the good luck to find you in town about the end of this month, where my stay will not exceed 3 or 4 days: mean time I remain

Your most Obedient Humble Servant

John Bowle

Northumbd. House June 2d. 1772

Dear Sir

I recd. your kind Letter, but could not get Avellaneda: there was an unlimited Commission given and
it sold for more than it was worth; wch. I was the
less anxious about, as I am promised a Copy from
abroad, & in the mean time have had the Book lent me:
wch. I have also procured leave to have lent to you,
and it is here with me ready to be sent you, if you
will favour me with a Direction by return of the Post
how it can be safely sent. Pray write immediately for
his Grace sets out for Spa next Tuesday (after wch.
time you must discontinue inclosing to me under his
Cover, but direct to me simply at Northumbd. House.)
As soon as he goes I shall retire to my Living in
Northamptonshire for the Summer. Pray inform me what
progress you make in your learned & ingenious Persuits
& esteem me constantly

Dear Sir

Your most faithful Servant

Tho. Percy

Easton Mauduit, near Castle Ashby
Northamptonshire, July 16. 1772

Dear Sir,

I should be extremely obliged to you if you could spare my <u>Romancero Español</u> 4to. and Cancionero 8vo. Send them up by some safe hand directed to me at Northumberland House, giving a Charge to the Porter to take care of them. --Please to send them as soon as possible.

Pray favour me with a long Letter, informing me what progress you have lately made in your Spanish Studies, & how you like Avellaneda; in return you shall hear more at large from Dear Sir

Your very faithful Servant

Thomas Percy

Excuse great haste

If you have any other of my metrical Spanish <u>Romances</u> or <u>Canciones</u>; send them also: I want none of my other Books. --When you write, do not inclose to the Duke who is at Spa: but direct to me simply at Northumbd. House; the letter will be forwarded to me.

Idmiston.   July.   28 1772.

Revd. Dr. Percy
Easton Mauduit near Castle Ashby
Northants.

Dear Sir,

I hope the books will come safe to your hands.
The Romancero has afforded some Illustrations, the
Cancionero none.   These as I have not at present time
to particularize, you will easily make out by the Pen-
cil strokes at the Index.   I shall just mention one of
Cervantes´s Ven muerte tan escondida wch occurrs in
his 2d. part C.38.   Perhaps these 2 are by the same
hand--Enamorado y Zeloso--Zeloso y Enamorado.   There
seems to be much of his phraseology in them.   I have
at length compleated the transcript of my Index near
700 pages, & made every extract for my purpose from
the Espejo de Cavallerias: This Historian is Merlins
Genealogist, & makes him hijo del Diablo.   Fresh matter presents itself -de la invencion del famoso Matea
[sic] Boyardo, whose Orlando Innamorato is a late valuable acquisition in my pursuits.   He copiously re-
lates the story of Brunello´s stealing Sacripante´s
horse wch. Cervantes mentions P.2 C.4 & wch Ariosto
just noticed in his 27th Canto.   You have satisfied
would I could add gratified my curiosity with Avellaneda: where every thing is to be condemned the sooner
we pass sentence the better: for my part I subscribe
implicitly to the Devils Testimony of the book in the
70th Cpter of the 2d. part of Q: & am certain that
what Mayans has said concerning it is true.   If to be
in every thing the reverse of Cervantes will entitle
the writer to any degree of merit He has a superabun-
dant share of it.   He has two novels I know not which
is most disgusting the silly Legendary story in one,

or the shocking Indecency of the other. In a word it almost refutes what Cervantes has twice advanced [II, 3; II, 59] -no ay Libro tan malo que no tenga alguna cosa buena. The only use I can make of it is that it in one or two Instances will occasionally explain some part of his Text, in every other respect tis too contemptible to merit any kind of notice, & is sunk into Oblivion against which it is not possible for all the art of man to buoy it up. I hope to return all your books when I come to town in December. Palmerin de Oliva stands ready for embowelling in which situation he has been for more than a twelve month past: I shall soon begin my operations on him. From a frequent attentive perusal of the Refranes of the Comendador Griego who is mentioned P.2.C.34 I find that there is much more Proverbial Diction in Quixote than is generally known. I do not recollect that I ever mentioned to you my Idea of a Map of Spain accomodated to the History. There are upwards of a 100 places named in it most of which I have had the luck to discover, but I have not yet to find the important <u>Puerto de Lapice</u> [I, 2; I, 8] which is doubtless some where in <u>La Mancha</u>, nor the river <u>Herradura</u> in Sancho´s pleasingly tedious Story to the angry Eclesiastico [II, 31]. I have much more to add upon this topick but Time compels me to bid you adieu. I remain

Your most Obedient H. St.

John Bowle

Northumbd. House Decr. 10. 1772

Dr. Percy´s Compliments to Mr. Bowle. He begs the
favour of his Company at the Chaplains Table on Monday
next, at a quarter after 3 o´clock. If Monday shd.
not suit then I beg the same favour for Tuesday.

24

London, Northumbd. House
Jany. 25. 1773.

Dear Sir,

I recd. the favour of your List of Spanish Books
wanted & forwarded it into France to my Friend, who
intended to go to Spain: But urgent business has
called him back to England, so that the opportunity
must be deferred. In the mean time he expresses a
great desire to be indulged with a Sight of Tirante el
Blanco and therefore if you could conveniently send it
up soon you will much oblige both him & me. You may
afterwards have [it] again when & for what time you
please.

I am going to publish Lord Surrey´s Poems, long
since printed off: and as he was the first who wrote
in English the Heroic Blank Verse of Ten Syllables (in
his Version of the 2d. & 4th. Books of Virgil, published first in 1557: ten years after his Death): I
wish you would collect for me some account of the In-
vention of that Metre among the Italians, (sc. by
Trissino, when, & in what works, &c. &c.) Your friend

Father Quadrio, will doubtless enable you to tell me all I want to know about it. Mention what other old Italian Poets used it: When & by what Spanish Poets it was adopted. --See Milton's Advertisemt. prefixed to his Paradise Lost, concerning Blank Verse: He does not seem to have known that any other Poet (except the Dramatists) ever used it before himself. --Yet there are one or two pretty long Poems in Blank Verse, written by Nicholas Grimald; at the End of Surrey's Poems, 1557. And a still longer Poem in the same Measure, among Gascoigne's Works, called the Steele Glass 1576. (See my Reliques. Vol. 2. pag. 136. 2d. Edit.) -- --
Besides these I do not recollect to have met with any other attempts in Blank Verse, sc. the Heroic Metre of 10 Syllables before Milton published his Epic Poem. I am,

Dear Sir

Your very faithful Servant

Thomas Percy

PS I know you will take so much care in packing up Tirante (as it is so fair a Copy) that I dismiss all solicitude on that head. Put a good deal of soft Paper next the binding. [...]

Idmiston Jany. 30 1773.

Dr. Percy
under cover to Duke of Northumberland
London

Dear Sir.

I wish I may not be too late in my present appli-
cation to you. There are two numbers in the last days
Sale of Mr. West´s Prints which I could wish to have
at a reasonable Price which I shall leave entirely to
your judgement: These are N. 48 Illustrium Artium
Hispaniae Tabulae, & N. 63 Effigies Sanctorum. Of
these last I want: Saints James, Paul, Martin, George
to adorn my Quixote: whom see P.2.C.58. Whatever
tends to throw light on the Geography of Spain may
have its use in our present pursuits. With this point
in view I have read with some degree of pleasure the
first part of a Viage de España printed the last year
at Madrid which I purchased of Elmsly. In the course
of his travels the writer has occasion minutely to
describe La gran cuesta Zulema [I, 29] (see V.2.139)
which he does in two places. This book may probably
merit your attention from the notice taken in it of
some valuable copies of pictures done at Rome para un
gran Señor Ingles, El Conde de Nortumberland, aficio-
nado, y protector de las bellas artes, que ordeno las
tales copias. Carta Octava. S.10. I hope the Refranes de Nunez in Davies´s Catalogue have not escaped
your ken. I am with particular Respect

Your much Obliged & Obedient Humble Servant

John Bowle

Northumberland House, Feb. 8 1773.

Dear Sir,

I am sorry to inform you that your Commissions came too late: I happened to be from home when your Letter arrived so that it did not reach my hands till the Auction was over. I am now going into the Country till next Saturday & hope to find at my return <u>Tirante el blanco</u> safely arrived in Town: I write in the greatest haste: but am with the greatest Regard

Dear Sir

Your very faithful Sirvt.

Tho. Percy.

Idmiston. Febry. 23. 1773.

To the same.
as per last.

Dear Sir.

I now sit down in good earnest to do what I have long desired, & that is the answer to that part of your letter respecting the Origin of Blank Verse among the Italians. [...]

No Original Spanish Poet of this sort occurrs:

only two Translators present themselves: The former
El Secretario Gonçalo Perez the Father of the Unfortunate Antonio in his Ulyxea de Homero, traduzida de
Griego en lengua Castellana, en Anvers. 1556. 8.vo.
His lines are generally twelve or thirteen feet. The
other is Francisco de Aldana who traduxo en verso
suelto las Epistolas de Ovidio. See the Vida de Cervantes, S. 115. But it does not appear that they were
ever printed. Tis plain both these took the hint of
it from the Antients. I hope long ere this Tirante is
safe arrived, as I put him into the hands of a trusty
Friend. I am, with great respect,

Your most obedient Humble Servant,

John Bowle

P.S. [...]

28

Northumberland House, March 24. 1774.

Dear Sir,

I cannot resist the pleasure of letting you know,
that I have procured the use of an Old Spanish Romance
for you, wch. is among those mentioned in Don Qui-
xote´s Library, but which I never could get sight of
before: --It is the Hist. of <u>Olivante</u> <u>de</u> <u>Laura</u>, lent
me by a Friend, with full permission to let you have
the thorough Perusal of it. Let me know how & when I
shall send it you: or if you are coming soon to town,
perhaps it may be as well to keep it for you to carry
back with you. I am, Dear Sir

Your very faithful Servant

Tho. Percy

PS I believe I can only be indulged in the loan of it
for you, for about 2 Months, but this will be fully
sufficient for you to give it a thorough Perusal. --
Inclosed I send you Proposals for a new (catch-penny)
Version of Don Quixote. It only shows one thing, viz.
that the Public is constantly awake to every new proposal relating to our favourite Author: which is en-
couragemt. to hope that we may make some effort our-
selves, with advantage. [The version of Don Quixote
is that of Charles Wilmot; the advertisement has been
reproduced in Journal of Hispanic Philology, 9 (1985,
publ. 1986), 184-85.]

29

Idmiston. March. 31. 1774.

To Dr. Percy.
Under Cover Duke Northumberland
Lond.

Dear Sir.

I am highly pleased with the prospect of perusing
any Book that promises to illustrate our Favourite Author. Olivante is I presume a bulky Gentleman, I know
not how else to account for the expression of Este
Tonel, which is applied to him [I, 6]; he is onely
once more mentioned & that is in the 20th C.P.1. It
was not till after I had taken my leave of you when
last in Town that I purchased the Diccionario de Madrid: This great work has furnished numerous Illus-

33

trations of the Text, which, without it, would to me have remained unintelligible. I will instance one, & that is P.2. C.3 Refran de paja, y de heno &c. el pancho lleno: which seems to indicate a charge of writing for bread. After frequent Perusals of the Refranes de Nuñez I have never been able to find this, & several others, among them, as was doubtless his own case, when the Dutchess said that Sancho´s were more in Number than those of the Comendador Griego. C. 34. The Solitary Satisfaction of the Philosophers EUPHKA is sometimes my case, particularly in any new discovery as lately happend in that of Benengelis exclamation on aquel gran Poeta Cordoves ib.ib.p.92 [II, 44]. This was Juan de Mena in his coplas. I cannot give over all thoughts of a Classical Edition of this great work, & should reluctantly make publick in a Translation what the Author perused in the Originals, which should be pointed out. The particulars respecting Brinelo, & his stealing Sacripante´s Horse are to be met with in Boiardo & Ariosto; I think I mentioned to you in a former Letter [No. 22] the omission of this remarkable circumstance both in Berni & the Espejo de Cavallerias. Be mine the merit hereafter to avail myself of the past drudgery of my Indexes, & poner las anotaciones y acotaciones in consequence of them, & believe me this has been frequently work enough; Be it yours in due time to give him an English Dress: Nor ought a Genius less than his that writ,

Attempt Translation; for Transplanted wit

All the Defects of Air & Soil doth share. How unequal to this Task must (the seemingly Pseudonymous) Wilmot be, who ascribes to the Divine Original Ludicrous Dialogues &c & Drollery, instead of what every where occurs Grave & Serious Irony, which by an Art peculiar to himself The Author has made the Vehicle of Morality & useful Instruction for the Conduct of Life. I shall be egregiously disappointed if I do not see you before St. George´s day, when I intend to return all your Books. Perceforest will afford but little for our purpose. One would think Arthurs Metamorpho-

34

sis into a Crow should be to be met with in Geffrey of Monmouth 'tis worthy of him, but whether it be so or not will be then ascertained when I see the book, which I have never yet. As I hope soon to have the pleasure of a Conversation with you I shall for the present put a stop to my pen by assuring you that I remain

Your much obliged & Obedient Humble Servant

John Bowle

30

Idmiston Febry. 11. 1775.

Dr. Percy.
under Cover to Duke of Northumberland
London

Dear Sir.

After the long suspension of that Correspondence which was ever highly pleasing to me in my solitude, I take the liberty to renew it by acquainting you with what I have been doing, & also to ask the favour of you to execute a few [s]mall commissions for me at Dr Askews sale. The work which has been so long in my thoughts, was every material wished for it at hand, which is very far from being the case, must necessarily be the result of time. Repeated readings are necessary: This occurred from a Late Instance in looking into Boiardo, where I found him mentioning Rinaldo's stealing a Mahomet from Marsilio, & which eluded my former ken:

                Sotto la tregua del Re Carlo Mano,
                Rubasti al Re Marsilio il suo Macone
                      Orl. Innamor. L. 1 C. 28 St. 7
D.Q. C.1. But there is no penance, no drudgery here,
rather new pleasure in the reperusal of this fine
Poet. This past summer I have read over several of
his countrymen with particular attention to Cervantes,
& have the satisfaction of having very frequently
traced out his allusions to them. I have gone thro
the dry desert of the many thousand lines of the Mor-
gante Maggiore of Pulci, &, fortifyd with a proper
share of Patience have traversed the less fertile &
more ungrateful soil of Alamanni in his Gyrone il Cor-
tese: In both I have discoverd that Cervantes went
this road before me. If some less pleasing, some disgusting objects present themselves in the two ample
atonement for their defects was made to me in the
bright scenes, & charming prospects which are at every
proper Interval dispersed by that fanciful Painter Il
Divino Ariosto. As he three times expressly names
him, so there are frequent direct allusions to his
Orlando. --The Tesoro Militar de Cavalleria, por D.
Joseph Micheli Marquez. Madrid 1642 Fol. after more
than six years quest is at length come to my hands, &
has abundantly answered my expectations. Tho he is
considerably later in time than Cervantes, many Historical passages in this book throw great light on
him. Monsieur de S. Palaye though a valuable writer
is not I think calculated for Spain. En cada tierra
su uso is a just proverb & particularly so when applied to Chivalry. One thing is observable in common
that every species of Knighthood participates of the
Andante--What is our Kings laying his sword on the
Cavallero Novel´s shoulder but the Espaldarazo of the
Ventero on Quixote [I, 3]? But there is not a circumstance there that may not be confronted with similar
instances in the Spanish Historians. Espero mediante
V. M. en buen ora ser el huesped de los tres famosos
Cavalleros Bernardo del Carpio, el de la Cruz, y Olivante. Ellos tendrán un buen acogimiento conmigo a

pesar del fuego del Ama. I coud wish it may be convenient for you to inspect the numbers at Baker´s which I have selected, & either purchase them yourself or leave my commission with him as will be most agreeable. I intend God willing to be in town some time next month, & shall have an opportunity of remitting him the money by the beginning of it when I know the event. Nos 688, & 695 will I make no doubt have their use in my searches, & if on viewing them you think I am too low go a step or two higher. I heartily congratulate you on the honours conferred on your noble family in the late Elections, to which I am much mistaken if you have not essentially contributed, as I think I discovered your Pen in one advertisement at least: & with my best wishes & thanks to you for your past favours remain

Your much obliged & Obedient Humble Servant

John Bowle

Dr. Askews Sale at Bakers Rev. Bowle wishes to possess:

No	Name			
474	Casas, (Barth: de las)	--3--	Sold for	2--6-0
493	Morga (Ant: de)	--4--		1-11-6
688	Caro (Rodrigo)	--7-6		0-12--
695	Marmol (Luys de)	1-1-0	Mine	1--2-0
792	Teixera (Pedro)	0-9-6	Mine	0--2-0

Northumberland House, Feb. 15. 1775

Dear Sir,

I recd. your obliging Letter of the 11th. Inst. and lost no time in examining the Articles you pointed out in Dr. Askew´s sale: I did not think, upon Inspection, that Nos. 474, 493, 792, deserved intrinsically more than you had marked them at, and therefore I have let your Prices stand: but Nos. 688, & 695, which seemed to be more for your purpose & were besides in very fair condition, I have ventured to mark a little higher, as you desired me, viz. 688 at <u>10:6</u> 695, <u>1:11:6</u>. --Thus altered, I have given in your Commission to Baker in my own Name & hope all, or most of the Articles will fall to you. --No. 493 tho´ of little intrinsic value, may possibly fetch a good price among the curious researchers into the Hist. of printing because this was produced from the Press in Mexico, & has a particular Memorandum of Dr. Askew´s on that Subject; but it seems to have little other merit, so I did not add to the price you had affixed. --Be assured, it gives me very great pleasure both now & at all times to execute any commands for you: and I really wish I could have attended the Auction myself to have bid for you: but alas! I am prevented not only by interruptions of various kinds, but by a swelling I have got in one of my legs in consequence of an ugly bruise recd. 3 months ago by a fall, which confines me very much to my Chamber.

I am happy at all times to hear from you, & interest myself too much in the success of your reasearches, not to rejoice that your Studies among the Italian Poets have turned out so profitable. I hope you will soon come to town & allow us to enjoy your Company here a little longer, than in former years

that you may be able during your residence in town to
run over "El Cavallero de la Cruz" --Bernardo del Carpio, -Las Lagrimas de Angelica; and El Cancionero de
Madonada [sic; ´López Maldonado´], the four scarce
books lent me by Mr. [Thomas] Crofts, & which (as he
is absent from England) I am not at liberty to let go
out of the Metropolis: --But as for Don Olivante de
Laura, which is my own property, he shall accompany
you to Idmerston, when you go back.

The 4 above-mentioned you will soon run thro´, &
then you will leave nil desiderandum on our favourite
author. Believe me to be

Dear Sir

Your very faithful Servant

Thos. Percy.

PS Don´t neglect to avail yourself of this opportunity
of perusing Mr. Crofts´s 4 Books, for fear at his return they should cease to be accessible.

32

Northumbd. House. March 11. 1775

Dear Sir,

On Tuesday last the Sale of Dr. Askew´s Books
ended; when the amount of the Sale turned out to be
about 4000 ll. which is 500 ll. at least more than the
most sanguine expectation suggested. --Of the Commissions you intrusted to me, the two following Articles
have been purchased for you. viz. --

No. 695, 3 vols. Descripcion de Africa

Ł s

1:2:0

792, Relaciones de P. Texeiro 0:2:0

They are both in fine condition & in my opinion extremely cheap. --I shall reserve them till you come
to Town & shd. have given you notice of them sooner,
cd. I have found your frank before wch. was mislaid.
I am, very truely

My dear Sir

Your faithful Servant

Tho. Percy

33

Idmiston. March 20. 1775.

To Ditto
as the last

Dear Sir.

I am truly thankful for your kind attention to my
commissions & am very glad they have turned out so
well, tho I cannot but wish that Rodrigo Caro had fell
to my lot: but paciencia y barajar: I must wait a
little longer. Marmol, & Jaime Bleda whom you possess
will I think afford abundant satisfaction for every
enquiry respecting the Moors. I had no particular
view to answer in the acquisition of any of the rest.
& the missing of them was no disappointment. --My
visit in town will be quite transitory in my way to
Cambridge & Norfolk where I intend to pass a fort-

night, & shall be so straitned in time that I cannot
stop more than one night which will be the 28th when I
hope to see you or early the next morn: I propose to
leave all your Books with your Porter as I come along
which will apprize you of my arrival: My future mo-
tions you will know better by word of mouth than by
writing.   I hope to find time to avail myself of the
use of your four Books [see no. 31], particularly Bernardo del Carpio.   He is five times named by Cervantes, & the only particular act of his is suffocating
Orlando at the Battle of Roncesvalles; this he mentions thrice V. 1 Lond. ed. p. 4, 264 V. 3 306 [I, 1;
I, 26; II, 32].   Amidst the many very high prices I
have no doubt from your account of the goodness of my
bargain.   For this & all other favours I remain

Your ever obliged & most obedient humble Servant

John Bowle

P.S. By mistake of the Post your Letter travelled to
Ilminster Somerset which retarded my answer.

34

Idmiston.   May. 22. 1775.

Mr. B.´s Complements to Dr. Percy, & acquaints him, by
means of his Friend Mr. [John] Ives, that one of the
Spanish Poets of prime note {see before p. 14 [i.e.,
letter to Percy of Feb. 23, 1773]} who used blank
verse was the famous Garcilasso de la Vega; an instance of which is his Epistola A Boscan, in the Madrid edition of 1622.   Fol. 49 & seq.   He has an odd
species of verse fol. 85 & seq. where the rhyme is
uniformly in the middle of the line [...]

Idmiston. March. 25. 1776.

Revd. Dr. Percy
at Northumberland House.

Dear Sir.

I still with my usual perseverance prosecute my great undertaking, of which I send you a specimen,* & hope in due time to complete the whole with tolerable success. To effect this, Good Luck threw into my hands a Book when I was last in Town to which I am more indebted for that knowledge which I think I have of the Spanish than to all others whatever. This Writer is Covarruvias. In him I possess a Tesoro della Lengua Castellana, o Española. I have not only occasionally consulted, but regularly went thro the whole of this Dictionary, & tho I was more than a month in my manuscript from it I have room to think much has escaped my Ken. From him I have learnt why Cervantes stiled the Knights Lady Dulcinea, & the meaning of her change into una villana de Sayago T.3.303 [II, 32]. While the great Dictionary [Autoridades] gives a meaning to words from Cervantes he gives us that sense which obtained in his time as they were Cotemporaries. I would not let Aldrete's Origen slip tho I bought it dear as I knew you wanted it. --I hope what I send will want no material change the rest I intend to bring with me next month. I am with great respect

Your most Obedient Humble Servant

John Bowle

* First 24 pages of A Letter to him concerning a new Edition of Quixote. [Bowle's footnote]

[The next communication between the two, as can be seen from the subsequent letter of Percy, was Bowle's publication, whose title page will be transcribed in full: A Letter to the Reverend Dr. Percy, concerning a new and Classical Edition of Historia del valeroso cavallero Don Quixote de la Mancha. To be illustrated by Annotations; and Extracts from the Historians, Poets, and Romances of Spain and Italy, and other Writers Ancient and Modern; with a Glossary, and Indexes. In which are occasionally interspersed Some Reflections on the Learning and Genius of the Author. With a Map of Spain, adapted to the History, and to every Translation of It. By the Reverend John Bowle, M.A.F.S.A. The title page bears the following quotation: "Miguel de Cervantes merite quelque distinction. S'il avoit eu l'honneur d'être un Ancien et que son Ouvrage eût été écrit en Grec ou seulement en Latin; il y a dejá long-tems qu'il auroit eu des Scholiastes et même des Commentateurs en forme. Avertissement à Tirant Le Blanc."

The Letter is much too long (fifty-six pages of text) to be reprinted here. It is intended as an announcement of Bowle's edition, to be published by subscription, and after arguing the need for "a classical edition," illustrates the type of annotation and indexing to be provided.]

Easton Mauduit, Feb. 3d. 1777

Dear Sir,

I ought long since to have acknowledged the very kind influence of your Friendship and the great honour done me, in your late curious Publication: of wch. I have been favoured with two Copies; For the first, which was left for me at Northumberland House above a Month ago, (just as I was leaving town) I intended to have thanked you the moment I got into the Country, but my attention has been here wholly engrossed by an Accident of the same Melancholy Nature, as that which proved so afflicting to me in Town: Having performed the last Offices to the good Duchesses of Northumberland, I hastened down to my country benefice; when a like misfortune befell the family of the Earl of Sussex here, by the unexpected Death of his Lady. As I am under great obligations to this noble Family, who were my first Patrons; I was obliged to assist in preparing for and in performg. the last Solemn Duties to Lady Sussex, & have by this & other pressing Avocations been most exceedingly engaged: which I hope you will have the goodness to accept in excuse for a Silence, which would otherwise have been extremely blameable after receiving such flattering Marks of Respect & attention, as you have paid me by your late learned publication: of which Mr. White has lately sent me a second Copy. --I have read it over again with great eagerness & heartily wish the Public may be excited to demand such a Classical Edition of our favourite Author, as you have pointed out, & could so perfectly execute. What a pity it is, that Lord Granville is not still living, or that his Editor Pineda was not possessed of your immense fund of Castillian Erudition, and indefatigable Diligence. I sincerely & ardently wish that your preliminary Performance which shows such an uncommon extent of Reading may meet with the general attention it deserves; but am much affraid, it will be Caviare to the Million; & that you must be content to gratify a Select Number of curious Readers, like myself who admire the excellent Cervantes & endeavour to relish him in his Original Language. Should my Fears in this respect, (which friendship for you excites) prove groundless, no one will more sincerely rejoice than,

> Dear Sir

> Your most obliged & very faithful Servant

> Thos. Percy

PS A Letter may be inclosed to me under a Cover thus directed (till they take away the Privilege of Franking) only be careful to insert the P for Distinction To P The Earl of Sussex at Easton Mauduit near Castle Ashby in Northamptonshire

I hope to be in London next month, & to hear that your Publication is very well received by the best Judges.--

38

Idmiston. Feb. 10. 1777.

Revd. Dr. Percy.
under Cover - To the Earl of Sussex
at Easton Mauduit near Castle Ashby
Northampton Shire.

Dear Sir,

I had just been reviewing El Verdadero Historia-
dor Turpin--che <u>mai</u> <u>non</u> <u>mente</u> in alcun loco, as Boiardo in one place expresses himself, or as he says in
another--che mai non <u>mente</u> di ragione, when the arrival of your Letter broke in upon my reveries, & made
me at once Sad & Happy-- Sad from my Impatience, before I got half-through it, & from my apprehensions
that you had a nearer loss than two such valuable
noble friends, Happy in hearing from you, receiving
your good wishes, & my own hopes that I have advanced
nothing that may disgrace either you or myself. I am
by no means indifferent as to the event of my proposed
scheme, & can have no doubt of success in the long
run: but this must not be prosecuted without some
present prospect: I have some promises, & am not
without hopes of properly introducing it to the world.
Mr Ventades the Spanish Consul has left a copy of the
Letter with the Prince of Masserano, & they have assured me that every assistance in their power shall be
chearfully given. I have by means of the former sent
another to Madrid to Don Casimiro de Ortega whom I
passed a day with in London, & hope to convey two or
three to Lord Grantham by his Chaplain Rev. Waddilove:
should my plan succeed, I have no doubt the work would
be admissible into Spain, which for many reasons Lord
Carterets could not. Although upon the whole my Labours will be principally for such as are conversant
in both the Spanish & Italian, yet it may induce several to commence an acquaintance with the original, as
the principal intent of the Annotations will be to
facilitate the knowledge of it. And now leaving the
Event to time, with my hearty thanks for your ser-
vices, I for the present bid you farewell, & remain

Your Ever obliged,

& Most Obedient Humble Servant,

John Bowle

[The following letter was published by John Nichols in <u>Illustrations</u> <u>of</u> <u>the</u> <u>Literary</u> <u>History</u> <u>of</u> <u>the</u> <u>Eigh</u><u>teenth</u> <u>Century</u>, VIII (London, 1831), 165-66. This volume is readily available, and therefore the letter has been transcribed from Bowle´s book of drafts, so that the small differences between the two texts may be seen.]

May. 11. 6 o´clock morn. 1777.

Dr. Percy
Northumberland House
London.

Dear Sir.

My chaise is just ready for departure, & tho I have staid so long here leave this city with regret, as I had not the pleasure of giving you my printed proposals, & a receit or two in person: but as I had not this happiness I take the Liberty to leave them for you. I am embarqued in a weighty business, but have my hopes I shall buoy up, & meet with a favourable Gale. This must be left to Time to discover. Should matters succeed to my wishes I should present you with my first Copy, at all Events you shall have one of the best paper. Inclosed are five receipts: {D 12. Ns. 2,3,4,5,6} shall I suppose them for Dr. Douglas, Mr. Steevens for whom I have transcribed some notes, & think I have more, Mr Tyrwhit, Mr. Collingwood, or any friend of yours that may fall in your way? Mr. Barington, who in the most friendly manner espouses my plan, has desired me to acquaint you that he goes out of Town to morrow, & does not return in a fortnight. With every good wish towards you I remain

Your much obliged Humble Servant

John Bowle

P.S.   Shall have an opportunity some time in Whitsun
Week to send you a parcel.

Has mislaid the Transcript of the notes {to Mr. Ste-
phens for his Shakespeare}.

40

Northumberland House, May 22, 1777

Dear Sir,

I lose no time in acknowledging your most obliging & most acceptable Presents: which I shall highly
value both for their own sake, & that of the giver.
--I have forwarded your Letter to Mr. Ventades & have
the pleasure to inform you that two of my Friends desire to be subscribers to your Don Quixote, viz.

Thomas Tyrwhit Esqr, in Welbeck Street
Revd. Mr. Cracherode of Christ Church Oxford

I cannot help renewing my Solicitation that you
would take a Voyage to Spain as you wd. examine that
Country with so much profit, both as to our favourite
Author, & so as to give us a far better account of
that Country than we have ever had: I only wish I was
at liberty to accompany you myself.   Adieu!   Believe
me ever

Dear Sir

Most sincerely Yours

Thomas Percy

41

[The first and formal part of this letter was published as "Remarks on the Word ´Romance´," Archaeologia, 5 (1779), 267-71. It deals with the linguistic
and literary meaning of the term, and is not reprinted
here. The second part was published by Nichols, Illustrations of the Literary History of the Eighteenth
Century, VIII, 169-70. As with the letter of 11 May,
1777, the text in Bowle´s book of drafts is edited.]

Idmiston. Oct. 27. 77

Revd. Dr. Percy
Northumberland House
London.

Sir

I beg leave thro your hands to convey to the Society my sentiments respecting the Word Romance [...]

Shall I have fought thro the whole Battle of Roncesvalles, & say nothing of the Event of the Engage-
ment to my respected Friend Dr. Percy? That be far
from me. Yes, Dear Sir, I have done this. With my
accustomed Perseverance I have toild, & turmoild thro
El verdadero Suceso de la Famosa Batalla de Roncesvalles, con la muerte de los doze Pares de Francia, por
Fr. Garrido de Villena. en Toledo. 1583. 4to Six &
thirty as dull & tedious cantos as ever merited Fire,
or perpetual Oblivion. If I have not in many instances traced Cervantes here, yet to make some amends

for my drudgery various Illustrations of his text have presented themselves from this Quarter. For this fatigue I am obliged to Mr. Mickle the Translator of Camonens. I do not recollect that I ever mentiond any thing to you of Don Casimiro de Ortegas letter to Mr. Ventades in which he mentions ´la nueva Edicion de Dn Quixote por nuestro Rev. Bowle, & adds ´ha parecido aqui grandemente, y linsongeado el gusto de todos los eruditos, y singularmente de la Academia de la Lengua Castellana, la Idea original de imprimir la obra de Cervantes con todos los honores de un Autor Classico, y la de añadir un mapa topografica [sic] del Itinerario del Heroe Manchego. --Ha tomado nuestro amigo el verdadero camino de interpretar, y facilitar la inteligencia de los passages obscuros, consultando los Romancero [sic] assi Italianos como Españoles, y otras obras antiguas à que aluden las expresiones de Cervantes. Io me intereso por el mismo Rev. Bowle en sus lucimientos, he consultado sobre el mapa al mejor Geografo que aqui tenemos &c, &c. & he is no other than Don Tomas Lopez, The publisher of the Atlas de España, who has corrected its numerous errors, which subscribed with his own _firma_ Don Casimiro for me. It is dated from Madrid in February last. I have lately had some friendly hints from the same Quarter thro Mr White, tho he did not acquaint me from whom they came. But a Letter to him from Rome of the first Instant from John Talbot Dillon Esqr. promises great things. The writer says, that having lived many years of his youth in Spain he acquired a most perfect knowledge of the Language, that he has by him a very large Collection of Notes critical historical with Illustrations of Don Quixote, explaining all the hard words & difficult passages, the whole being the result of near twenty years study & two journeys into Spain & Portugal, & desires to know if the same would be agreeable to him or the Ingenious Author in Question. I have answerd his Letter, & thanking him for his offer have closed with his proposal, giving him an abstract of what I have done. inclosing my proposals & map & hope

50

to hear farther from him when I come to town, which
most probably will be very early in December. I have
not been slothful in my searches this past summer but
tho I have been much at home, have travelled thro
France & Italy to get acquainted with El Señor Escoti-
llo one of whose disciples was the fabricador de la
cabeça encantada, & find him to be not, as his name
Seemd to impart, a Scotch, but an English Conjurer. I
hope the Elegie on Cleeveland will be as acceptable
now as when you last heard from me, at which time I
had mislaid it. I remain Dr. Sir

Your much obliged & Obedient Servant.

John Bowle

42

Northumberland House, Novr. 8. 1777

Dear Sir,

        I recd. your very obliging Letter & truly rejoice
at all the good that befals you: The pleasing Prospects that open upon you from Italy & Spain, give me
as much Pleasure as they can do to yourself: They
promise you most valuable acquisitions: and you deserve every assistance: I beg to hear from time how
you proceed. I admire your Patience & honour your
Diligence with regard to El verdadero Suceso &c. I
have picked you up a Subscription for two Copies since
I wrote last wch. I desire you will add to your List.
viz.

        The Revd. Mr. Dutens, Rector of Elsdon in
        Northumberland, 2 copies

This gentleman is at present abroad but he has told me
he will be answerable for 2 Copies.

Let me now return you my best thanks for your
most acceptable Present of the Poem in Praise of
Cleiveland: Nothing could have been to me more desirable: Any thing hereafter on the subject of him or
any Percy will be most desirable to

   Dear Sir

     Your most obliged & faithful Servant

     Thos. Percy

PS Shall not I have the pleasure of seeing you in Town
next Month, during my waiting at St. James's: How
happy shd. I be to be favoured with your company at
the Chaplain's Table.

      43

      Idmiston. Jany. 1 1778

Sir.

  At the time I am solving your difficulties I am
informing myself. I shall begin with those passages
you gave me in the order they occur in the Book: &
first Sancho's wish T. 1. 189 [I, 21] --quiera Dios
que Oregano sea, &c. You will not be surprized when
you are told that he alludes here to this Proverb.
Plegue a Dios que oregano sea, y no se nos vuelva en
Alcaravea. The meaning of which, as appears from the
Great Dictionary, is that as some harm was to happen,

it might not be very great. The Dutchess is not so
complaisant to Sancho, as you will see by comparing
what she says to him in her use of this same Phrase
P.2 T.4. 33 [II, 36] which is the only place beside
this where the word is to be met with in the book.
The Sobras del real Same Tome & Chapter p. 193 [I, 21]
refers to the Transaction mentioned before p. 167
lines 6,7,8. Violent Metaphors are sometimes to be
met with in Cervantes as we shall see presently. This
may be one of them & as the azemila fue bien bastecida
de cosas de comer he might [unfinished]

44

[Edited from British Library Additional MS 32329, ff.
97r-98r.]

Idmiston. Aug. 17. 78

Dear Sir.

I cannot but with the highest satisfaction impart
to you the pleasure & Information I have received from
the ever valuable correspondence of my Friend Mr. Dillon. I may justly stile him such from his representa-
tion of my undertaking in Spain. I have received
three Letters from him, since I had the pleasure of
seeing you, all repleat with matter pertinent to the
same. He visited Barcelona a principal scene of ac-
tion in the History of the Knight, Tarragona, & the
Royal Convent of Poblet, where he was hospitably en-
tertained three Days, & where he spent many hours in
their Library in searching for me, but without success. At Valencia he formed an acquaintance with Don
Gregorio Mayans y Siscar, who made him the first visit, & at his house presented him with several of his

53

works: to him he mentiond my scheme, who added it
would give me immortal honour & shame to his countrymen. An accident of his Servant prevented him from
visiting Toboso. What he could not discover at Poblet
concerning the Cid <u>quando</u> <u>quebro</u> <u>la</u> <u>silla</u> <u>del</u> <u>Rey</u>
[Part I] C.19. He has explained copiously in a manu-
script of an old Romance at Madrid, which begins--<u>A</u>
<u>concilio</u> <u>dentro</u> <u>en</u> <u>Roma</u>, which possibly you may find
in some of your Cancioneros. An Acquaintance of his
[Juan Antonio Pellicer] is publishing a collection of
Tracts, & Among the rest <u>Noticias para la vida de Mi-</u>
<u>guel de Cervantes Saavedra</u>, of which he has inclosed a
specimen, & which if it appears before he leaves Madrid he shall bring with him as a present to me from
the Author, & if not, will send by another conveyance.
I shall expect from hence abundance to gratify my curiosity in this important particular. Mr. [Edward]
Collingwood's Copy [of the 1608 edition; see letter
no. 48] has been of infinite utility to me, I print
from it & very generally prefer the readings of the
text to those of the other copys, unless I find some
reason to use them: In this Edition there are some
very material Additions, & Alterations, & some judi-
cious defalcations, all of which will appear in the
<u>Varias</u> <u>Lecciones</u>. I cannot but surmise that this was
corrected by the Author himself, tho´ as far as I can
find no use has ever been made of it: I will not hes-
itate a moment to say no good Edition of the text can
ever be had without it. I hope to receive more written, & much oral information from my friend when I
have the pleasure of an interview with him, & particularly the event of one pursuit, which I named to him
on your account, that of King Arthur. In his last
letter dated Madrid June 20th he tells me, I am in
quest in the royal Library of his being turned into a
crow &c the success of which you shall know when I
arrive in England, which I hope will be towards the
end of August. But now I have mentioned this, I shall
refer you to your Friend Mr. Barington who cites from
the Laws of Howell Dda this passage -- Tres sunt aves

quas in fundo alieno occidere non licet -- et cynus &
corvus p. 334 [?] H.7. The Decretum Aureum (rectius
plumbeum) Domini Gratiani Parisiis. 1506. Fol. F.333
furnished the Siquis suadente Diabolo &c of the 19th
Chapter which I had been years in quest of. I am so
far advanced in my great undertaking that I have all
hopes in due time to compleat what I have so long had
in contemplation. Harvest, Quixotism, & gloom,
brightend sometimes by the arrival of some kind Epis-
tle -- nec gratior ulla est Quam sibi qua Percy sub-
scribit Littera nomen are the present objects of my
attention. I am, Dear Sir,

            Your ever obliged, & Obedient Humble Servant

                        John Bowle

P.S. I have just received a friendly Letter from a Mr.
[Francis] Villion, who I understand is known to you,
on the subject of my work.
I must with Mr. [Topham] Beauclerc´s leave some time
or other run over Haedo´s Topografia de Argel.

                        45

                  Alnwick Castle, Aug. 29th. 1778

Dear Sir,

      I am truly obliged to you for the kind favour of
your Letter, & for the very agreeable Account of the
progress of your Discoveries. Interested, as I am, in
the Success of your Work, any Information on that Subject will ever be peculiarly acceptable to me. You
have met with a treasure in Mr. Dillon; to whom I beg
you will always remember my particular Respects: &

this not only on account of the honour I had of his acquaintance, when in England; but for the valuable assistance he affords you on our favourite Subject.

You will very much oblige me, by continuing to impart to me from time to time your future Discoveries, as leisure & opportunity suggest. I am only sorry that I must continue an idle Spectator of your curious Researches, without being able to advance them. --What a valuable assistant will you gain in Don G. Mayans y Syscar, if it be only to consult occasionally that able Philologist, on points of Criticism. --I am exceedingly glad that Mr. Collingwood´s Edition proves so useful: He called on me at Northumbd. House, to pay into my Hands a Subscription, which he had recd. for you: but I had left Town & therefore he paid it to Mr. [Tom] Payne at the Mews-Gate for your use; as he has since told me: for I have seen him since I came into the North; & shall let him know, when I see him again, what you say in your last.

May I request a favour of you wch. at once requires attention & Secrecy. A friend of mine is much interested in the health of your Dean of Salisbury. --Will you have the goodness to favour me with a particular Account how he does: & if he should die, transmit the earliest Account of it, by an immediate Line directed to me at Northumbd. House London; without inclosing it to the Duke. In this you will highly oblige

Dear Sir

Your very faithful Servant

Thomas Percy

PS Will you pardon me the Want of a Frank? The Duke has the Gout in his hands & I have very unfortunately left in London the Frank you gave me.

[Edited from British Library Additional MS 32329, ff. 103r-v.]

Idmiston. Nov. 12. 1778.

Revd. Dr. Percy
Northumberland House.

Dear Sir,

No very particular news from Sarum [Salisbury] premised, Your Friend must expect a little longer. I saw the Dean a few days ago, & he looks just as well as he has this summer, which has been very poorly, he has in a manner lost his appetite & is going for Bath.

I will now come to my own concerns, & shall begin with a transcript of a Paragraph from Mr. Dillons last letter of Sept. 29 as it immediately concerns yourself. 'I am greatly obliged to Dr. Percy for the favour of his kind remembrance, & when next you have an opportunity of writing to him, you will do me a particular favour if you will please to present my respects to him, & that I hope to have the honour of presenting them in person next winter at Northumberland House, when I shall also wait on Lord Algernon Percy who honours me with his Protection, & with whom a few years agoe I spent a very agreeable winter at the Court of Vienna.

I have just now received a specimen of the good effects of his most friendly interposition in my concerns in a letter from Madrid [of Juan Antonio Pellicer; missing] of which I here inclose a copy, & when you have satisfyd your own curiosity, let me beg the favour of you to send it by the Penny post, as directed. The book mentioned which the Author has sent me

is Ensayo de una Bibliotheca de Traductores Españoles
[of Pellicer], & is just now imported by Mr. White:
Besides the Vida de Cervantes it is repleat with Literary Information concerning Spain. I wished to give
you the earliest notice about this matter if you
should choose to have it. I have thankd Mr. Collingwood by Letter for his Favour, & hope before the 10th
of next month to have the pleasure of seeing you & Mr.
Dillon --a painfull pleasing interview this! With a
man who has been so sincere in his Friendship to an
utter stranger --For I can no more doubt of this,
than of the reality of his several accounts, which
have this additional recommendation, that I know them
to be true, & for which I am his very grateful debtor.

I remain

Your ever Obliged Humble Servant

John Bowle

47

Northumberland House
June 13, 1780

Dear Sir,

Inclosed is the List you desired me to make out,
of subscribers thro´ me to your curious Edition of Don
Quixote. This inclosed Paper contains all the names I
at present recollect. I hope you are going on with
vigour & hereafter one may hope to collect more. --
The late Riots (thank God) seem happily terminated:
Peace & tranquility are restored. I am preparing to
go to Carlisle on friday, & wish you a pleasant Sum-

mer. Believe me to be,

Dear Sir

Your very Faithful Friend & Servant

Tho: Percy

Subscribers to Mr. Bowle's Edition of Don Quixote

The Earl of Aylesford.
Sir Grey Cooper Bart.
Thos. Tyrwhitt Esq.
Geo. Steevens Esq.
Revd. Dr. Vyse.
Revd. Mr. Dutens 2 Copies
Revd. Mr. Cracherode
Dr. Percy, Dean of Carlisle.

Query, the following:

Honble. Daines Barrington
          I believe he desired to be a
          subscriber.

48

[Edited from British Library Additional MS 32329, ff.
116r-117v.]

Christchurch. July. 28. 1780.

Revd. Dr. Percy
at Northumberland House
London.

Dear Sir.

As I presume from your last favour that you are now seated at your Deanry, I flatter myself that I shall be no unwellcome intruder there, as you have probably more leisure minutes than in town. Duly sensible of your good offices I inclose you a specimen of my labours. [In Bowle's draft he has noted that the enclosure was "Anotaciones Sheet 9."] Many uses have arisen to myself, & of course to my future readers from the numbering the lines of the pages: Hence I have been enabled to prefer one place to another, & with more precision & propriety agreeable to the Authors hint poner Las Anotaciones y Acotaciones. This is the case of nunca fuera Cavallero: where in the second part [I, 13] the allusion is much larger than in the former [I, 2], & the reference to the page & line will gratify the curiosity of the reader much more fully. By this sketch you will see what use I have made of the books you lent me. Of these & every other I propose to have an A.B.C. with references to their several Quotations. The transcript of my notes for the press, in which I am advanced as far as Chap.14.P.2. frequently furnishes me with surprize & astonishment as they arise out of a Chaos, & inevitable confusion from their being inserted, either in the interleaved copy, or elsewhere, at very different, & distant periods: Of course they have as much novelty to myself as to any other reader, some of them being wrote ten or eleven years back. I hope I do not impose upon myself when I assert, that no one can understand Cervantes fully that does not come to my school. Who can be said to know him well, who is unacquainted with his Obligations to the Italian Poets? Who among his numerous readers has any Idea of this? The inclosed sheet has but little of it, but the characters of el Cura, el Oidor, y la Pelea in the 45th Chapter of the first part will appear in double lustre when confronted with the several passages from Ariosto: & the great Genius of Boiardo seems transfused

60

into Cervantes from the happy use he made of him in Sancho´s perdida del Rucio, & which he has himself pointed out in the fourth chapter of the second Part. El Nilo llano p. 93 1. 9 ["el libio llano," I, 14] is the indisputably true reading which nowhere occurs but in the Edition of 1608, Mr. Collingwoods copy. The Note de los Yangueses [I, 10; I, 15] is literally Mr. Dillons. One use of the references is the avoiding repetitions, so that it is apparent that one note will illustrate very remote passages as you will see by turning to 83.7, 84.29, 86.1, 88.7, 108.2. & so of the rest. That my searches have been very general is most apparent. Lord Grantham in a conversation with Mr. Dillon at Madrid, & which he mentioned to me in one of his letters from that place, seemd to think my views confind to the Libros de Cavallerias: but the perusal of these forms but one, tho a great & essential part. Cervantes tis most certain was no superficial scholar, but intimately acquainted with antient as well as modern litterature. I could wish my scheme to be placed in a proper light to his Lordship, as hoping it would merit his notice. To have missed Mr. Tyrwhits book would have proved a real misfortune, as it contains those Romances which the other Cancioneros wanted. There is a reference to it 97.22 as well as to your Silva. I am not more obliged to him for the use of his book, than for his polite & friendly manner in communicating it to me. He told me that he had mentioned it to Payne, & that he desired him to acquaint me with it, which was forgot. I had also two interviews with Dr. Johnson, at the first I left with him the whole I had printed with the first sheet of the Anotaciones, to which he expressed some objection as being separate from the text: but acquiesced at length from its being not practicable to place them in the usual manner. He had heard of my undertaking, was civil, & obliging, & wished to see me when I came to town again. When there was a prospect of your travelling westward I had thoughts, & they have not quite left me of saying something to you of the Episcopus

puerorum of Salisbury, which being, as I remember from
a slight glance in your House book mentioned to have
been at Beverly, I had some reason to think came down
from thence. Not having an opportunity to consult
that Authority I desisted. I have hopes of making my
publick entry at the end of the present, or Beginning
of the next year. May you live many & happy: and Fare
well, if you never make tryal of any of the Receits in
the Forme of Cuny [?], of my Friend with whom I now
am, & who greets you well. I remain

        Your ever obliged & most Obedient Humble Servant,

                        John Bowle

[P.S.] Mr. Barington was among my first patrons.

                            49

[Publication of Bowle´s edition, early in 1781.]

                            50

                                    6 June 81.

    Dr Percy leaves his best compliments for Mr.
Bowle & begs leave to mention that he shall set out
for the North at the very beginning of next week wishing very much before he goes to receive his favourite
Don Quixote either on Saturday next or Monday morning
at Northd. House.

Carlisle, Dean´ry July 15 1781

Dear Sir,

In the List of Subscribers to your excellent
Editn. of Don Quixote I forgot to mention one to you,
who I find paid into my hands his first subscription,
of ₤1 11s 6d. This was Apr. 15, 1778, John Lewis
Boissier Esq. ₤1 11s 6d, to whom I gave a Receipt of
yours numbered D.12. No. 2. -- I hope you will excuse
this omission and send to Northumbd. House for the
Money. --Mr. Boissier is a Gentleman, who resides
much at Geneva, but often comes to England & the first
time he does so I shall probably see or hear from him,
when I will remind him of you. However, if you please
you may address a Card to him mentioning that I had
paid his first subscription into your hands & desiring
to know how you may transmit the books to him & receive his second subscription, Direct A Monsr. Monsr.
Jean Louis Boissier, Gentilhomme anglais, a Geneve.
[...]

I hope you will think of my proposal of printing
an additional Volume or two, containing all the Metrical Romances & Epitomes (at least) of all the Prose
Stories, which are quoted or referred to, or (at
least) necessary to understand our favourite Author.
Wishing constant success to your useful and ingenious
Studies, I remain

Dear Sir

Your faithful Servant

Thos. Percy

P.S. [...]

Index of People and Books

Because the letters deal with <u>Don Quixote</u>, and refer frequently both to books Cervantes knew and to literary contemporaries of the writers, the opportunities they present for annotation are limitless. My emphasis has been on identifying the Hispanic books, authors, and other allusions. Further information on matters discussed in the letters may be had from the other Bowle correspondence in the Bowle-Evans collection, summarized by Cox in <u>An English</u> "<u>Ilustrado</u>," Chapters V and VI. For an introduction to eighteenth-century English bibliophilism and comments on some of the collectors mentioned in the letters, see Seymour de Ricci, <u>English Collectors of Books & Manuscripts (1530-1930) and their Marks of Ownership</u> (1930; rpt. Bloomington: Indiana University Press, 1960), Chapters V and VI.

I have tried to avoid duplication of material easily available elsewhere. Specifically, for authors and books mentioned in <u>Don Quixote</u>, where one can turn to annotated editions for information, the first or most significant reference in <u>Don Quixote</u> is given, specifying, after the abbreviation "DQ," part and chapter. Recommended annotated editions for this type of bibliographic information are those of Bowle, Diego Clemencín (most readily available in the edition of 1966, Editorial Castilla, Madrid), Rudolph Schevill and Adolfo Bonilla y San Martín (Madrid: the editors, 1928-41), and the "nueva edición crítica" of Francisco

Rodríguez Marín (Madrid: Atlas, 1947-49). The best annotated translation is the revision by Joseph Jones and Kenneth Douglas of the translation of John Ormsby (New York: Norton, 1981).

Modern spellings are used. Reference is to letter number, not to page.

Willie Hunter, Bert Davis, and Barry Taylor have been generous in help with the identifications.

66

Barrington, Daines, 39, 44, 48. Observations on the
More Ancient Statutes from Magna Carta to the Twen-
ty-first of James I, first edition 1766. In
Bowle's Green Book there are seven letters to him,
1782-86.
Beauclerk, Topham, 44.
Beighton's sale of books, 18, 19, 20.
Bernardo del Carpio, 30, 31, 33. DQ I, 6.
Berni, Francesco, 29. Sixteenth-century Italian poet.
Bleda, Jaime, 33. Author of Crónica de los moros de
España, 1618.
Boiardo, Mateo, 22, 29, 30, 38, 48. DQ I, 6.
Boissier, Jean Louis, 51. In Bowle's Green Book there
is a letter to him, 14 August 1781.

Caballero de la Cruz, 30, 31. DQ I, 6.
Caballero del Febo, 19. Name of protagonist of Espejo
de príncipes y cavalleros by Diego Ortúñez de Cala-
horra, 1555; fictitious author of a preliminary
sonnet to Don Quixote.
Camões, Luís de, 41. DQ II, 58.
Cáncer y Velasco, Jerónimo de, 7. Obras varias, first
edition 1651.
Cancionero, octavo, 21, 22. Unidentified.
Cancionero de Madonada, see López Maldonado, Gabriel
Cancionero de romances, Mr Tyrwhitt's book of romances
mentioned in letter 48. From the "Autores citados
en las Anotaciones" (Bowle's edition, III, pp. xv-
xxi) we find that this was the edition of Antwerp,
1555. The copy in question was bequeathed by Tyr-
whitt to the British Library (C.20.a.36).
Canciones y Romances, a little old Volume of, see Silva de varios romances.
Caro, Rodrigo, 30, 31, 33. Author of Antiguedades y
principado de la ilustrísima ciudad de Sevilla,
1634.
Carolea, La, 7. DQ I, 7.
Carteret, John, first Earl Granville, edition of Don
Quixote (London, 1737-38), 17, 37, 38.
Casas, Bartolomé de las, 30, 31. Sixteenth-century

bishop; famous defender of rights of new world Indians.

Cavallero de la Cruz, see Caballero de la Cruz.

Cleveland, John, 41, 42. Seventeenth-century poet.

"Code of Spanish Laws," 6. Probably the Recopilación de las leyes destos reinos, various editions from 1569 to 1723, or the Nueva recopilación, 1743.

Collingwood, Edward, 39, 44, 45, 46, 68. A letter to him, 12 November 1778, is found in Bowle's Green Book.

Comendador griego, 22, 25, 29. DQ II, 34.

Cooper, Sir Grey, 47.

Covarrubias, Sebastián de, 35. Seventeenth-century lexicographer.

Cracherode, Clayton, 40, 47. Eighteenth-century bibliophile.

Crescimbeni, Giovanni Mario, 6. The work alluded to must be his Istoria della volgar poesia, first edition 1698.

Crofts, Thomas, 31. English bibliophile; Bowle bought some of his books upon his death in 1781. See Pedro M. Cátedra and Víctor Infantes, Los pliegos sueltos de Thomas Croft, Valencia: Albatros, 1983.

Davies' books, catalog of Thomas, 25. A London publisher and bookseller. In Bowle's Green Book there are three letters to Davies, 1772-82.

Decretum Aureum Domini Gratiani, see Gratianus.

Descripción de África, see Mármol.

Díaz, Rodrigo, Consejos políticos y morales, 7. The Rodrigo Díaz in question has not been identified. A book with the title Consejos políticos y morales, by Juan Enríquez de Zúñiga, was published in Cuenca in 1634 and reprinted in Madrid in 1665, according to Palau y Dulcet.

Diccionario de Madrid, see Autoridades.

Dillon, John Talbot, 41, 44, 45, 46, 48. English Hispanist; see Introduction, note 2.

Douglas, Dr. John, 39. Bishop of Salisbury.

Dutens, Rev. Lewis, 9, 10, 42, 47.

Effigies Sanctorum, 25. Unidentified.
Elmsly, Peter, 25. A London bookseller, one of those
at whose shop Bowle´s edition of Don Quixote could
be purchased, according to the title page of the
second printing.
Espejo de caballerías, 22, 29. DQ I, 6.
Espinosa, Nicolás, 8. Segunda parte de Orlando [fu-
rioso], first edition 1555.
Esplandián, Sergas de, 6. DQ I, 6.

Febo, see Caballero del Febo.
Felixmarte de Hircania, 18, 19. DQ I, 6.
Garcilaso de la Vega, 34. DQ II, 58.
Garrido de Villena, Francisco, author of Verdadero suceso de la famosa batalla de Roncesvalles, 2, 8,
41, 42. This book is commented on in the annotations to Don Quixote, I, 6, although I believe that
this traditional identification of Cervantes´ allusion is mistaken. (See Nicolás Espinosa in my "La
biblioteca de Cervantes.")
Gascoigne, George, 24. Sixteenth-century English
poet.
Geoffrey of Monmouth, 29. His twelfth-century Historia Regum Britanniae is the origin of Arthurian
literature.
Graal, Old History of the San, 15. Probably L´hys-
toire du sainct Greaal, Paris, 1516 or 1523.
Grantham, Lord, 48. Thomas Robinson, second Baron
Grantham, English ambassador to Spain 1771-79.
Granville, see Carteret.
Gratianus, 44. Gratian´s Decretum or Decretum Aureum
is a fundamental work of canon law.
Great Dictionary, the, see Autoridades
Grimald, Nicholas, 24. Sixteenth-century English
poet.

Haedo, Diego de, 44. Author of Topographía e historia
general de Argel, 1612.
Historia de Fray Gerundio [de Campazas], see Isla.

69

Homer, Odyssey translated by Gonzalo Pérez, 27.

Illustrium Artium Hispaniae Tabulae, 25. Unidentified.

Isla, Francisco José de, 15. Eighteenth-century satirist.

Ives, John, 34. Researcher on English antiquities, 1751-76. In Bowle´s Green Book there are seven letters to him, 1773-75.

Jackson, Mr Andrew, bookseller, 1, 6. Jackson is discussed by Brooks in the article cited in the Introduction.

Johnson, Samuel, 48. The great lexicographer and man of letters.

Kelly, George, translation of Don Quixote (1769), 12.

Lágrimas de Angélica, Las, see Barahona de Soto, Luis.

Lambrechsts, Juan, Ramillo o Guirnalda de discursos políticos y éticos (1656), 7.

Leacroft, Samuel, 19. Publisher of Percy.

Lepolemo, see Caballero de la Cruz.

López, Tomás, 41. Spanish geographer; editor of the Atlas geográfico del Reino de España; first ed. 1757.

López Maldonado, Gabriel, 31. DQ I, 6.

Mariz, Pedro de, 7. Diálogos de varia historia; first ed. 1594.

Mármol Carvajal, Luis de, 30, 31, 32, 33. Mármol´s Descripción general de África (Granada, 1573-99) is found in the catalogue of Bowle´s library, as is his Historia del rebelión y castigo de los moriscos del reino de Granada (Málaga, 1600).

Masserano, Prince of, 38. A member of the Ferrèro-Fiéschi family.

Mayáns y Siscar, Gregorio, 2, 6, 8, 9, 22, 27, 44, 45. Author of first life of Cervantes, commissioned for the edition of Carteret, translated into English by

John Ozell (qq.v.).

Mena, Juan de, 29. Fifteenth-century poet.

Menezes, Fernão de, Vida e acçoens d'el rey Dom João I (1677), 7.

Micheli Márquez, José, 30. Seventeenth-century Spanish author.

Mickle, William Julius, 41. Translation of Lusíadas of Camões, Oxford and London, 1776.

Milton, John, Paradise Lost, 24.

Monmouth, see Geoffrey of Monmouth.

Morga, Antonio de, 30, 31. Author of Sucesos de las Islas Philipinas, 1609.

Ninfas [y pastores] de Henares, 3. DQ I, 6.

Northumberland, Hugh Smithson, first Duke of, 4, 5, 12, 14, 17, 19, 21, 25, 29, 30, 45.

Núñez, Hernán, see Comendador griego.

Old Reliques, see Reliques of Ancient English Poetry.

Oliva, see Palmerín de Oliva.

Olivante de Laura, 28, 29, 30, 31. DQ I, 6.

Ortega, Casimiro de, 38, 41.

Osborne's catalogue, 10.

Ovid, 27.

Ozell, John, 8, 9. Translator of Cervantes and other French and Spanish authors, d. 1743.

Páez Viegas, Antonio, Principios del Reino de Portugal (1641), 7.

Palmerín de Oliva, 19, 22. DQ I, 6.

Paterson's, sale of books at, 14.

Payne, Tom, 48. A London bookseller, one of those at whose shop Bowle's edition of Don Quixote could be purchased, according to the title page of the second printing.

Pedigrees of most if not all of the Spanish nobility, A large thin folio MS. containing the, 10. Unidentified.

Pellicer, Juan Antonio, 44, 46. The collection in question is Pellicer's Ensayo de una biblioteca de

response to him are conserved in the latter's Epis-
tolarium.
Virgil, 24.
Vyse, Revd Dr William, 47. Rector of Lambeth.

Webb's books, Philip Carteret, 14.
West's prints, sale of James, 25, 26.
White, Mr B., bookseller, 37, 41, 46. Four letters to
him, 1774-78, are found in Bowle's Green Book.
Bowle's Letter to Dr. Percy was "printed for"
White, whose shop was also one of those at which
Bowle's edition of Don Quixote could be purchased,
according to the title page of the second printing.
Wilmot, Charles, translation of Don Quixote (London,
1774), 28, 29.

Contents